When you've got a thing to say,

Say it! Don't take half a day...

Life is short...a fleeting vapor.

Don't you fill a whole blamed paper

With a tale which, at a pinch,

Could be cornered in an inch!

Boil her down until she simmers,

Polish her until she glimmers.

Advice to Writers
Joel Chandler Harris

Table of Contents

EFFECTIVE BUSINESS WRITING:

TIGHT AND RIGHT

R. KARL LARGENT   EARL L. CONN

Robin Vincent PUBLISHING

Effective Business Writing: Tight and Write

R. Karl Largent and Earl L. Conn

Robin Vincent Publishing LLC
2829 Grand Avenue
Davenport, IA 52803

First Printing: 1999

Library of Congress Card Number: 99-067973

ISBN: 0-9645606-3-1

Table of Contents

Table of Contents

Table of Contents

Table of Contents

PREFACE

Methods of communicating come and go. Who can say how we will transmit business information 10 years from now, even five years from now? But one thing remains certain: Whatever the method, the ability to prepare that information clearly and in a readable format never will change.

That's what *Effective Business Writing: Tight and Right* is all about. We have one goal. That goal is to accelerate your continuing preparation for better business writing. No matter where you or we stand in this field, we can always learn more about doing it better. Both authors have been in the writing business for decades, but it's accurate to say we learn every day. Sound like an exaggeration? Believe us, it isn't.

This workbook is a step in that direction. It's divided into four parts.

Part I, "Getting Ready to Write," emphasizes the crucial point that thinking needs to precede writing. Writing is mostly like the rest of life. The better prepared you are before you start, the more success you can expect. So thinking about what you're going to write is critical.

Part II, "The Mechanics of Writing," frankly, may be more than you want to know right now about grammar and language usage. But it's there if you need it. We've tried to stick to the basics.

Part III, "Internal Documents," and Part IV, "External Documents," are built around our thesis that the special difference in these two is audience, not writing style. What does the audience already know? What is your goal in reaching this particular audience? These are the questions that matter.

In this extended edition, we have put "Practical Practice Drills" in every section. You can immediately put to work the skills and insights you are learning as you go along. You will find "Solutions" in the back of the book. You will also find the book contains many "Write Tight and Right Tips" which help summarize.

Following our thinking that we are always learning, we equally are interested in your comments about *Effective Business Writing: Tight and Right.* We welcome your suggestions for improvements or needs not sufficiently addressed. And thank you.

Earl L. Conn
R. Karl Largent

PART I

GETTING READY TO WRITE

"Less is more."
Robert Browning

What's Happening Here?

You are about to embark upon an interesting, informative, and style-changing journey. It's a journey in which you will learn to think about some very old writing and business communications practices in some different, and, we hope, enlightening ways.

If you are like most people, a few years back, perhaps even more years than you care to remember, you sat through your English or grammar classes. You hated or, at best, tolerated a teacher who presented boring material you saw no need to assimilate. So you probably did one of three things:

1. Became bored to the point of distraction.
2. Were mildly intrigued but totally befuddled by all those rules of grammar.

(Who cares if my participle dangles?)

3. Casually wondered what difference all those rules really made when you stepped out into some world other than the classroom.

Correct?

Well, one of two things probably happened then:

1. You learned to muddle through fairly well without really mastering any more writing skills.

Or,

2. You figured, what the hey, so I can't write. I

wasn't planning to be Stephen King anyway.

So, what happened?

Lots of things. You went off to school, studied harder than you ever thought you could, earned yourself a degree in marketing, accounting, engineering, or what have you; turned out to be bright and promotable; and all of a sudden you have assignments and responsibilities you never dreamed possible.

You are managing people, dollars, and projects. You're firing off all kinds of correspondence: memos to co-workers, letters to customers, and reports to superiors. In fact, there are days when it seems like all you do is write. And you're the one who figured that it didn't matter much one way or the other whether you mastered this thing called "writing."

But it doesn't end there.

When you're not doing all of the above, you're being asked to evaluate members of your staff for promotions and salary increases. It means even more writing.

Your boss tells you, "Write a performance review."
"Work up your unit's business plan for next year."
"Give me a full report on the Miller acquisition."

When those are done, you construct, analyze, and summarize, from Heaven knows what sources, for people who determine your level of contribution by what you write.

By now, you're thinking that maybe you should have planned to be Stephen King because you seem to be doing more writing than he does.

Welcome to business writing in the '90s.

Some of you may even be at that point where you believe the old adage, "You are what you eat," should be changed to "You are what you write."

Scary stuff, huh? Particularly for someone who didn't do all that well with those earlier English drills and not much better in those college composition courses.

Help Is On The Way

That's why we're here. That's why we've developed the *Effective Business Writing: Tight and Right* workbook. We believe *Effective Business Writing: Tight and Right* can help anyone get a better handle on this whole business communications process.

Anyone?

Well, almost anyone.

How do we do it? We do it by showing you a different way to think about the business writing process. We present you with a new way of looking at what you write and how you communicate.

One person said, "Look, I didn't like writing classes in high school or college. They were boring. What makes you think it's going to be any different this time around?"

It is not our objective necessarily to make you enjoy writing. Our objective is to make you proficient enough to survive in today's business environment.

We have noticed something about people who are insecure about their communication skills. If you ask them to write out the solution to a problem, they will begin, almost immediately, to scribble out some sort of poorly constructed response.

By the same token, if you ask these same people a question, they are quick, often eager, to respond. But their response is usually laced with a series of hems, haws, throat clearings, and poorly thought through answers.

Same problem, different skills. Why is this the case?

Answer: Organization.

And where does *organization* come from?

In the communication process, it comes from thinking about what it is you are going to say or write before you actually begin to utter words or jot them down on paper.

Hearing this *think before you do* step in a business writing class a couple of years ago, one of the students came up with a reply that caught us off-guard and provoked some very serious thinking.

"l like what you're saying," the young man said, "but I want you to think about how I've been taught up until this point in my life. Starting with the first grade, and all the way through high school, I've been told what to think. Looking back, I cannot think of a single class where the emphasis was put on me developing my ability to think my way through to a solution."

Isolated incident? Probably not. When this story has been repeated to subsequent classes, the students in almost every case have confirmed what that young man said.

Thinking – What Do You Mean by 'Thinking?'

We would like you to think about why we've been talking about *effective business writing*. We aren't talking about just plain *business writing*. What needs to happen in the course of a hectic business day is a great deal more than just sitting at your desk churning out any number of written documents.

For equally obvious reasons we're not talking just about *effective business speaking* or *effective business listening*.

We speak of *effective business writing* because *writing* means systems of conveying information involving more than one method of delivery. To us that means we talk, listen, think, evaluate, comprehend, react, cooperate, and, hopefully, accomplish something as a result of that exchange we call the communication process. Effective business communication needs each of these facets to achieve its objectives.

EFFECTIVE BUSINESS COMMUNICATION SKILLS

1. Verbal Skills   4. Writing Skills
2. Listening Skills   5. Comprehension Skills
3. Cooperation Skills 6. Assessment Skills

David Harper, president of D.H. Harper and Associates, a major management and communications consulting firm, points out that basic verbal and listening skills are required for even the most elementary levels of performance within the business structure.

He goes on to say that cooperation is also vital at this level of contribution.

Basic skill levels of 1, 2, and 3 don't do much more for an individual than make him or her eligible for employment.

Adding competency in effective writing skills, the fourth essential skill, immediately separates this individual from a performer with only the first three attained proficiencies. "When we are talking about skill level 4 and up," Harper explains, "we are talking about abilities that have to be developed in order to advance through the management levels."

Developing and mastering comprehension and assessment abilities are equally critical, but they are beyond the scope of this discussion. Like the four initial levels, they are vital to operating effectively within the business environment.

If you haven't already discovered this fact, you will soon learn that a business is an entity unto itself. It is a community within a community, a culture within a culture. In order to achieve objectives within that community and culture, you must communicate effectively with your superiors, your peer group, and with equal effectiveness with your subordinates. A shift leader who cannot motivate his production team is in a heap of trouble. It is difficult to motivate when you haven't honed your communication skills.

Having said all of that, let us give you just one of many acceptable definitions of effective business communications that we will be discussing. It's in this "Write Tight and Right Tip," one of many offered in this book.

Write Tight and Right Tip
EFFECTIVE BUSINESS COMMUNICATION MEANS DEALING WITH PEOPLE IN A WAY THAT ENABLES YOU TO ACCOMPLISH MUTUAL BUSINESS OBJECTIVES AND ACHIEVE MUTUALLY AGREED UPON BUSINESS GOALS.

By now, someone either reading this workbook or hearing the above for the first time, is saying, "Hey, it isn't just business. Writing and communicating effectively are essential in every facet of any organized activity."

So true.

Improve your writing and communication skills and you will see the positive impact in other dimensions of your life.

But, for the moment, let's focus this brief look at writing and the totality of the communication process by saying that, for business purposes at least, *effective business writing* is more than just jotting down or uttering a few words, even though they be brief, relevant, and to the point. It is the sum total of a lot of things, all of them beginning with thinking.

Communication is listening to what was said, knowing why it was said, understanding what was said, and then doing something constructive with the information.

By the same token, effective communication skills give us a way to respond to that input with positive output, either verbally, in writing, or in some other positive form of action.

Let us sum it up this way.

1.   Within the constraints of the organization, communication, usually written, is the way goals and objectives are defined.

and

2.   Well-developed communication skills, particularly writing skills, are essential to progress, both personally and for the institutional entity.

Write Tight and Right Tip

THE ABILITY TO COMMUNICATE EFFECTIVELY IN WRITING IS A SKILL. SKILLS ARE DEVELOPED. AS WITH ANY SKILL, THE MORE YOU PRACTICE, THE MORE PROFICIENT YOU BECOME.

First You Think, Then You Write

Now that you have a better concept of the place writing holds in the overall communication scheme and within the organizational structure, let's take a moment to do a little self-appraisal of your writing skills. Answer the following questions by assigning a numerical value to each answer. The numerical values range from 1 to 10. The number you assign indicates how you feel about your current writing abilities. Give yourself a 10 if you feel the question addresses an aspect of written communication that you have mastered. If you feel that you need work, but do understand the basic concept of the question, you may want to consider awarding yourself a 6, possibly even a 7.

On the other hand, if you feel inadequate at your present writing skill level, you may decide to give yourself something closer to a 3 or 4.

Seldom do we see a 10, which is someone who knows everything there is to know about effective written communication. Nor is it likely that there are any 1's in attendance. In theory at least, a 1 could not handle even a basic writing assignment.

While you are completing the questionnaire on the next page, you might be keeping in mind the kind of writing skills required of you in your present capacity within the organization and the necessary level of writing skills to seek advancement in your present organization or to seek employment elsewhere. After all, those present requirements and where you're trying to go are really the point.

Practical Practice #1

1. I rate my overall writing skills as a_____.

2. I rate my skills as a communicator as a _____ .

3. My punctuation and spelling rate is _____ .

4. My vocabulary rates a _____ .

5. I always stick to the point_____ .

6. I never ramble when I write_____ .

7. I never have trouble expressing myself_____ .

8. I always organize my thinking_____.

9. I know where to start_____ .

10. I know how to wrap it up_____ .

11. I know how much background to give_____ .

12. I am always certain about format_____ .

13. I'm comfortable with my writing style_____ .

A perfect score, of course, would be 130. If you gave yourself a 130, close this book and head for the ballpark. You have either overrated your communication skills, or you are one-in-a-million. In either case, this workbook can't help you. Essential to improving your written communication skills is recognition of the need to improve.

If you gave yourself no more than 50 points or so, we'll have to throw in a few basics about grammar, punctuation, and basic writing along the way. But we planned to do that anyway.

The Plan

Fact: All writing must follow a plan.

If you stop to think about it, you'll realize that any piece of writing that actually gets something accomplished has achieved its objective because it followed a plan (a prescribed course of action). When we say plan, we are not referring to a formula. We are referring to a plan where:

1. You intend to say a specific thing about something.
2. You say the specific thing about that subject.
3. You review to make certain that's what you've said.

Those three very simple points are what we're talking about when we use the term, a writing plan. Let's talk about each of these points in more detail.

Point 1 asks what specific thing do I intend to say?

Let's take the example of someone who has decided to write a brief comment on how to throw a ball. Having decided on the topic, the person immediately launches into a lengthy description of how to grip and throw a ball.

Perhaps you see the problem.

1. Who is the reader and what do I, the author, expect the reader to do with the information I am about to give him or her?
2. Why am I writing this document? Do I expect something specific to happen as a result of what I write here?
3. How much do I know about this subject? Equally important, how much does my audience know about the subject?

Go back to the subject we said we were going to write about: throwing a ball. Consider Item 1 of the plan. Is my reader a child who knows nothing about throwing a ball? Or is my reader a high school athlete who knows quite a bit about the subject? It makes a difference where I begin, doesn't it? But even more basic is another question. What kind of ball am I talking about?

Why? We throw a medicine ball differently than we do a football or a baseball.

The bottom line is that before you start to write, you must have a plan.If you are going to write effectively, the first consideration in that plan must be your audience.Why? Because your audience dictates how much background information you have to include in what you write. Furthermore, your audience dictates the level of sophistication in the language you use. Your audience dictates the degree of familiarity with the subject matter or how guarded you must be in what you reveal. If location, location, location are the three most important considerations in real estate, then audience, audience, audience are the three most important considerations in developing an effective business writing style.

Okay. Let's turn our attention to Point 2: Why are you writing this document?

You do have a purpose, right? What is it? Do you expect someone to take some course of action because of what you write? Are you conveying a set of instructions? Are you asking someone to do something? Do you want someone to give you information? Whatever the case, your purpose for writing a document should be abundantly clear to the person who receives it. If there is any doubt in the person's mind, then you have not done an effective job of communicating.

Finally, consider your perspective in this communication

situation. Do you know more about throwing a ball than the person who is going to read it? If not, why are you writing it? Do you now suddenly realize that you really don't want to write about throwing a ball. Actually, what you really want to write about is the physics involved in throwing a curve ball.

When you stop to consider how much you know, how much your audience knows, and what you are trying to accomplish in writing, you are thinking. If you are thinking, you have started planning how you are going to handle this particular writing assignment.

Planning, then, is thinking about what you are going to write, how and why you are writing it, and, finally, what you expect to achieve by writing it.

Remember, in business as well as any other arena where writing takes place, any document you author should have a purpose. Even if that purpose is nothing more than giving vent to your creative juices, it is a purpose. If it doesn't have a purpose, maybe you aren't writing. Maybe you are just doodling.

Practical Practice #2

EXCEPT FOR GRAMMATICAL AND PUNCTUA-
TION DRILLS, MORE THAN ONE WAY EXISTS
TO CORRECT OR IMPROVE THE MATERIAL IN
ALL THE EXERCISES THAT FOLLOW. IN OUR
"SOLUTIONS," WE OFFER ONE. YOURS MAY,
OF COURSE, BE BETTER. IF YOURS IS SIMILAR
TO THE IMPROVEMENT WE RECOMMEND,
WE ACCEPT IT!

In the next few pages, we will make the distinction — a crucial one — between *internal* and *external* documents. For the moment, let's simply note that internal documents go to an audience likely to be already familiar with the subject in general and with the terms used.

Here's the Practical Practice event: A rapidly developing blizzard already has dumped five inches of snow. Management decides to send all personnel home at 10 a.m. The message is e-mailed to every office and telephone calls also made. The final sentence in both the e-mail message and the telephone call is, "We will inform you later how the hours will be handled."

The next day, most personnel are back. Now, how the blizzard-day hours will be handled needs to be communicated. The decision is that professional employees who were at work and were sent home will be paid for the hours they were scheduled to work. Personnel not scheduled to work will not be paid for any hours. Union employees will be paid for the hours they were scheduled to work and in addition will be paid for the hours actually worked until 10 a.m. Union employees must complete a "Work Record and Absence Report" to receive pay for the hours actually worked.

1.   In your situation, who would you expect to read this message and what would you expect these readers to do with the information?

2.   Is it clear why you are writing this document? Would it have been handled better by some other form of communication?

3.   How much would your readers know about the information you are distributing? How can you make certain that what your readers know and the information you give them will be sufficient for them to respond accordingly?

The Content

All business writing must be accurate.

The next consideration (after planning the who, what, why, and how of your document) is content. Since this is about effective business writing, the first thing that we are going to deal with is facts.

There are few situations in business where a document's need for accuracy is surpassed by the need for creativity or imagination. Not in place of but surpassed. Obviously, there are cases where that happens, but it is the exception rather than the rule.

So how do you find those facts?

Let's start with the premise that there are always two sources for reliable information (facts):

1.   Internal.
2.   External.

It just makes sense that in the process of creating effective business communications, you would start with what you can learn from your inside sources. After all, who should know more about your business than the people who live it and deal with it every day?

Logically, then, if you need information about some matter that is germane to the corporation or other business entity where you are employed, check with internal sources first. If at all possible, go to the source of the information. That person may be just down the hall or in the next office.

Let's go back to our ball-throwing example. As we suggested earlier, one of the things you may wish to explain is how a ball can be made to curve. That inside source may be the physicist who can explain why a ball curves if you throw it in a certain fashion. Now you have one set of facts.

On the other hand, your outside source may be someone you know who is capable of throwing a ball that curves. Don Drysdale, now deceased but a former pitching great for the Brooklyn and Los Angeles Dodgers, once described how he gripped the ball to throw a curve. Another Dodger great, Carl Erskine, now an Indiana banking executive, later described how he threw a curve. His method was completely different from the method used by Drysdale.

Which is the correct way? Both? Neither? Each?

Since each has Hall-of-Fame statistics to back up his preferred method, an effective business writing style would dictate that you report both methods of throwing a curve ball. Secondly, you would not permit your bias or writing style to report or imply anything other than the fact that both pitchers had highly effective, if entirely different, ways of throwing a curve.

To put it another way, to produce solid, effective business writing, your content must be unbiased and accurate. If your document is well planned and well constructed, and the content is accurate, you're off to a good start.

Write Tight and Right Tip

TO BE EFFECTIVE, YOUR WRITTEN COMMUNICATION MUST HAVE WORTH-WHILE CONTENT, A CLEAR AND READ-ABLE STYLE, GOOD FORMATTING, AND BE WELL ORGANIZED.

First You Think, Then You Write: Summary

Long before you start to write, there is one critical step you must take in order to insure effective business writing. You must plan.

One of the most common causes of ineffective writing results from the fact that too many people author a document without giving it adequate thought.

What are you going to say?
Who are you going to say it to?
Why are you going to say it?
Does it need to be said?
When does it need to be said?
Why does it need to be said?
How much do you know about it?
How much does the person reading your document know?
Do I have enough information about this?
Is the information accurate that I do have?

It's a fact. If taking the time to answer these questions frustrates you or if you willingly admit that you don't have the answers to each and every one of these questions, you are not ready to write the document.

Worthwhile Content

What do we mean by worthwhile content?
At a basic level, we mean whether or not it's worth

reading.

It better be. In fact, any time anyone in any business organization sits down to churn out any piece of business writing, the first question has to be why the author is taking the time to put this document in writing?

Let's talk about a simple thing like the cost of a one-page memo.

Step 1.   Mr. Gunther, the office manager, identifies a problem. For our purposes, any problem will do.

Step 2.   Mr. Gunther decides to inform his office staff of the problem. This information will be disseminated by means of the most basic internal document, the memo.

Step 3.   Mr. Gunther either drafts or dictates a memo to his secretary.

Step 4.   Mr. Gunther's secretary prepares a memo and returns it to him for his signature.

Step 5.   Mr. Gunther approves the memo, initials it, and instructs his secretary to disseminate it.

Step 6.   Mr. Gunther's secretary goes to the copy machine, makes five copies, and posts the memo on three office bulletin boards. She then puts one copy in her retained file of Mr. Gunther's memos and another in her central filing system.

What's the cost of all of this? Who knows? It depends on wage rates, OMO burdens, administrative costs, or whatever tag the controller puts on such procedures. But you can bet your bottom dollar that what we have just recited is a very expensive drill in communication.

In 1990, the ASMA, American Systems Management Association, estimated that in most American businesses the theoretical cost of a memo was somewhere in the neighborhood of $150.00. One wag suggested that maybe it would have been cheaper for Mr. Gunther to just ignore the problem. We doubt it. Most problems end up costing us something and often that cost is sizable.

Nor are we suggesting that a memo is an inefficient way to inform people of a problem.

The caution is: Don't sit down to crank out some sort of business epistle without weighing whether or not that document is the most efficient and effective way of doing it.

To a large extent, your purpose in writing the document is going to dictate your content.

So, what's your purpose?

Do you want to give someone new, convoluted, or confidential information?

Do you want someone to do something as the result of receiving your document?

Do you want someone to respond at a certain time, on a certain date?

Whatever your purpose — recording information, requesting action, soliciting involvement, directing the efforts of others — that document must have worthwhile content.

One seminar attendee claimed that no matter what he tried, his efforts at interoffice communications fell on deaf ears. "Nothing seems to work," he lamented.

"Do you draft what you are going to say?" he was asked.

"Sure do," he said. "I quote facts, figures, cite sources.

I give them all the information they need. But sometimes I think I'd get farther talking to a brick wall."

At this point, he was asked if he had a copy of one of his "ineffective" communiqués with him. It just so happened that he did. He was gracious enough to let us copy (verbatim) that memo:

The Memo

To: DataServ Personnel
From: Personnel
Subject: DataServ Smoking Policy

Effective with the posting of this memo, DataServ will institute a company-wide "No Smoking Policy." Smoking will be permitted in certain designated areas only. (See attached chart for areas where smoking will be permitted.) Persons found to be in violation of this policy will be reprimanded under the conditions set forth in DataServ SOP 66-10A.

Aside from the obvious flaws in this memo — no date, unsigned, not directed to a specific individual or department, or being issued by any individual — this memo is an example of not having worthwhile content.

A DataServ employee who discovered this memo posted on the company bulletin board should have many questions. Example: In one sentence the memo claims to be introducing a *company-wide No Smoking Policy.* In the next sentence, it says, *Smoking will be permitted in designated areas only.*

Which is it? *No smoking* should mean no smoking: not any, never, nothing, no part, no where, no how. But in the very next sentence we're talking about exceptions: *certain designated areas.*

While the above is confusing, the rest of the memo is worse. *Persons found to be in violation of this policy will be reprimanded under the conditions set forth in DataServ SOP 66-10A.*

What? More precisely, what is *SOP 66-10A?* And after you tell us what it is, tell us where it is. We'll concede, someone may know. But every reader?

Then tell us if some, many, or all of DataServ's employees have any clear idea what this unknown person, who signs himself *Personnel*, is talking about.

If I'm not a smoker, the whole scenario is funny. It's another example of management ineptness. Once again, it's the people in the front office getting things screwed up.

If I am a smoker, it's not funny, it's confusing. Personnel, whoever that is, is sending me mixed signals. Plus, I don't like being threatened.

In this particular case, the author of the memo quickly admitted he could have done a better job of explaining this policy to DataServ employees.

Worthwhile content boils down to making certain, once it is determined a written document is the selected way to present the information, that the content accomplishes its goals.

But pause for a moment. Stop to consider the communications problem of letting a number of employees know about a change of policy. What is the best way to do it? If you did not issue a plant-wide memo or bulletin, how would you handle it?

Would an announcement over the intercom work?

What about putting a notice in pay envelopes?

What about sending a letter to the homes of employees?

How about a personal phone call to each employee at home?

How about a series of meetings in which the new policy is discussed?

Obviously, there is a readily recognizable shortcoming in each of these alternative methods. Some are ineffective, some are not feasible, and some are too costly. Perhaps some combination would be the most effective communication.

In this case, while our DataServ personnel officer has considerable cleaning up before he can call it an effective memo, he did make the correct choice in format. A memo is the correct way to go. But if that memo is going to be effective, then more attention will have to be paid to its content.

Worthwhile Content: Summary

When we ask the question, *Does it have worthwhile content?* we are simply asking, *Is it worth reading?* Is whatever the document covers worth writing about in the first place?

The second question is about your purpose for writing this document.

Do you want to give someone new information?

Do you want to update someone on your progress?

Do you want someone to do something as a result of receiving your document?

Do you want to list facts for the record?

How much does your audience already know about the particular situation?

Do they already have background information?
Do you have to outline the situation before you start to discuss it?
Is document confidentiality specific?
Will this document generate the desired action?

Write Tight and Right Tip
ANY TIME YOU AUTHOR A DOCUMENT, YOU MUST CONSIDER WHETHER OR NOT IT IS THE MOST EFFICIENT AND COST EFFECTIVE WAY. WHILE YOU ARE CONSIDERING THAT, WE CAN SAY WITH CONFIDENCE: IN MOST CASES, A WRITTEN RECORD IS NECESSARY OF ACTION AUTHORIZED, INSTITUTED, OR REQUESTED.

Logical Organization

Assuming your document meets the first criterion of worthwhile content, let's turn our attention to logical organization.

Boil this second aspect of effective business writing down to its simplest elements and you have:

1.   An introduction.
2.   An elaboration.
3.   A summary.

The introduction consists of your telling the reader

about the document. This is the place where you state the problem, the premise, the opportunity, or whatever it is you expect this piece of writing to define or achieve.

Everyone has heard that old marketing adage that goes:

First, I'm going to tell you what I'm going to tell you.
Then I'm going to tell you.
Then I'm going to tell you what I told you.

This is called the First Principle of Reinforcement. The First Principle of Reinforcement applies as much to effective business writing as it does to marketing or any form of passing on information. The introduction in any document is the *First, I'm going to tell you what I'm going to tell you* portion of your document.

As a rule of thumb, the introduction — probably the first paragraph — in any kind of business writing should be brief and to the point. Go back to look at the last few documents you authored. Was the introduction brief and concise? Did it state the reason for authoring the document in the first place?

If you're having the slightest bit of trouble comprehending this concept of brief, let us give you some of these rules of thumb.

RULE #1. The introductory paragraph of a one-page memo should be no more than two sentences in length. It should go without saying that those two sentences should be as tightly written as possible. For documents of a longer nature (two or more pages), the introduction should be a short paragraph, probably four or five sentences at the most.

RULE #2.   Try to keep your sentences around 12 to 15 words. If you are authoring sentences much longer than that, you may be over writing. An occasional 25- or 26-word sentence doesn't necessarily mean you have writing diarrhea, but it should be the exception in length rather than the rule.

RULE #3.   The second element of logical organization is the central text of your document. This is the *Then I'm going to tell you*, or Second Principle of Reinforcement.

If there is a problem, this is where you define it and indicate what needs to be done.

If this document is presenting new information, this is where you explain it.

If you are presenting a problem, this would also be the area where you request your reader's involvement in the solution or whatever course of action you are proposing.

In other words, the purpose of your document and what you are proposing should be clear after the reader has read the middle portion of your document.

RULE #4.   In the elaboration portion (the place where you detail and discuss the purpose for writing the document), you give the reader an overall view of the topic.

Example: "The erosion of our customer base continues. ..."

Now you may wish to amplify this information with a few why's such as

"...this erosion could be result of less population in our target marketing area because of last year's flood."

and

"...the economic impact resulting from many of our traditional customers being unable to meet last year's market commitments. ..."

It is imperative for the reader to understand exactly what is happening here.

First, the author told the reader that he was going to discuss a problem. The author of the document even went so far as to outline the problem: "...the continuing erosion of our customer base."

Then, at some point in the second paragraph, the author of the document gave the reader more information. This knowledge is more in depth than the information contained in the first paragraph. Another way of looking at it: The author is presenting the document in layers.

RULE #5. Each succeeding paragraph should give the reader additional information or immerse the reader further into the purpose of the document.

When you have said everything that needs to be said (Note. We did not say, "Everything you want to say"), you bring your document to a conclusion by summarizing it.

The summary, like the introduction of the document, should be tightly written, specific in direction, and void of generalization. "I will expect your response no later than..." or "Please give this matter thought and get back to me by..." or "Your input will be appreciated. If it looks as though all your data won't be in by the due date, advise me no later than..."

RULE #6.   Be straightforward. Be specific in your directions. Make certain the readers know what is expected of them. Ambiguity has no place in business writing.

Practical Practice #3

Edit the following sentences. Remember, in general, sentences of about 12 to 15 words make for the easiest read.

1.   Jimmy walked across the bridge, following the girl in the red dress, and then he stopped when she paused at the gate of the large house.

2.   While I was explaining to the girl that the lesson was not as difficult as she seemed to think, her eyes began to fill with tears and soon her body was racked with sobs.

3.   Tom, Jim, Betty, and Sally were going to the movie,which they had been told was to start at 4:15 p.m. but, on arrival at the theater, they found the earlier movie had started late and the new starting time for their movie was instead 5:15 p.m., an hour's difference.

4.   The cousins took their sleds up to the top of the hill, swung them around to face down the long slope, got on their sleds, pushed off and started down, gathered speed as they passed the old oaken tree, turned them to miss the long culvert, and then glided to a stop just before they came to the creek which was swollen with water run-off from the new, heavy snow.

5.   While he believed that she should take the job if she really wanted to, he was hesitant to say too much because she might think he was trying to unduly influence her decision which he didn't want to do even though he did have his own opinion about her taking the job.

Logical Organization: Summary

A well-organized business document has an easily recognizable introduction, a complete and informative elaborative text that explains the problem or situation, and a summary detailing what action the author expects.

RULE #1. The introductory paragraph for a one-page memo should be no more than two sentences long. For a longer internal document, no more than four or five tightly written sentences.

RULE #2. Sentences 12 to 15 words in length are the most effective and easiest for the widest range of readers to comprehend.

RULE #3. The second part of your document is your central text, where you make your purpose clear.

RULE #4. In the elaboration (middle) portion of your document, the author directs the writing from a broad description or discussion of the overall opportunity, issue, or problem, down to the finer points or aspects of the matter. This practice gives the reader an overall perspective before discussing minute points.

RULE #5. Gradually immerse the reader in the document by delving (successively) into deeper and deeper issues as the text progresses.

RULE #6. The summary should reaffirm expected action and spell out due dates.

Tight Writing Drill

Examine the following memo. In light of what you now know concerning logical organization of a document, does this memo meet the criteria for good and logical organization?

THE CROSS BOW MEMO

DATE: 9/09/99
TO: Jan Hawkins
FROM: Carol Manning
SUBJECT: Cross Bow Investigation

As it now stands, we are four weeks behind schedule in completing the initial phase of this investigation. According to the timetable established by the bureau director, Sara Hanson, in Kansas City, we should be completing the third phase (the internal audit) this week. The third phase of the project is currently less than half complete. The external   audit is likewise behind schedule, and as of this date, the project leader, Dan Hennings, cannot give me a completion date. It was due to be completed one to two weeks ago. The coordinators of both the internal and external audits blame their lack of progress on the fact that they are operating shorthanded. Hanson is recommending that we meet in her office no later than Friday. Check your schedule and let me know if that works for you.

Ask yourself...
Does this memo meet the format criteria established on the previous pages? What about sentence clarity and length?
Does the memo conclude with an expected action statement?
If the memo, as written, doesn't meet our expected criteria, how would you rewrite it?

Practical Practice #4

REWRITE THE CROSS BOW INVESTIGATION MEMO
HERE:

_____

_____

_____

_____

_____

_____

_____

_____

_____

_____

_____

_____

A Clear and Readable Style

In business writing classes, the majority of students tend to stare back in disbelief when they are told that much of what they learned in that basic composition class just doesn't apply in the halls of the corporate world.

Why?

For one thing, most expressive writing or composition classes do not teach the kind of writing required in the business community. Of course, that's why many academic institutions have developed business writing courses.

Let's back up a step to explain.

In today's society, most of us are faced with communication not only on several levels but with writing that must meet several different needs.

Without elaborating, people today often write to fulfill the need to record certain aspects of their life. Diaries, personal journals, family chronicles, etc., are all popular. This is called *personal writing*, and the truth of the matter is that no one much cares how you do it.

Another type of writing is what could be called *minimal social writing*. This is the stuff of the social-pseudo business world. It's your letter to your insurance man protesting the rate increase, the church or charitable organization report, a letter to the editor of your newspaper, a letter of complaint to your congress person, or maybe an article for your local newspaper.

Then there is a third field of writing, the one that most of us are familiar with — if for no other reason than it is the one stressed by so many teachers — *expressive writing*. It's the stuff of lower level composition courses.

Finally, there is the *writing of the business community*.

Don't describe the sunset. Tell me what happens when the sun sets. This is a world of facts. Some conjecture too, but only when it is requested.

While it is true that most of us are called upon to write in each of these social arenas at various points in our lives, it is equally true that the writing we do in each will not likely satisfy the requirements of the others.

Having said that, let's get a little closer to this word *style*.

Style is not what you write. It is how you write it.

Style is form, not content.

Style impacts the quality of your written communication,

and . . .

Style can make you effective or ineffective when it comes to written communications in business.

Voltaire said, "Any style that is not boring is a good style."

Let us paraphrase Voltaire, "In business writing, any style that gets the job done is a good style."

Style Tips

In defining the do's and don'ts of effective business writing, the three cardinal sins are:

1.   Verbosity.
2.   Sesquipedalianism.
3.   Wordiness.

VERBOSITY is simply the practice of being too pretentious and too flowery.

As the flaming sphere of burnt orange descended into the azure blue waters of the Gulf, a dream-like magenta haze drifted over the water, enveloping me in a surreal world of enchantment, causing me to forget the passage of time.

Forty-one words. Not the stuff of business writing.

Given the same information to be written for business purposes, the savvy business writer would have written something like this: *The sunset was so enthralling I forgot about time.*

Nine words. The writing of business. Brief. Concise. Timesaving. Economical. Accurate.

SESQUIPEDALIANISM becomes evident in your writing when your written communication efforts indicate you are trying to dazzle your readers with big words.

There are two problems with sesquipedalianism:

a. People shouldn't have to have a dictionary handy when they wade through some document.

b. Sesquipedalianism should be reserved for games of impress and counter-impress. It is ineffective and not good communication.

Here's an example. Suppose someone is asked to describe what happens to a group of people sitting in a downpour at a football game.

If the person responds that the fans were *permeated with precipitation* or *moisture laden,* that person is being sesquipedalianistic. On the other hand, if the person says nothing more than *the people got wet,* the communicator leaves a bit to be desired.

Why not say, *The people got soaked* and give the reader a solid description of exactly what did happen. *Soaked* gives the reader far more information than wet. Agree?

WORDINESS is more of a problem for people who fancy themselves good communicators than folks who feel that their communications skills need improvement.

Take the following example:

Being wordy means you are writing unnecessarily long, ungainly, tedious sentences that may appeal to you but simply read as overwritten to your reader. (24 words)

Or it could be written:

Long, ungainly sentences are difficult for everyone. (Seven words and darned if it didn't say the same thing.)

Take the word *certainly*. You hear it all the time. What do you do when you hear it? You nod, yes. Despite the indefiniteness or impreciseness of what the person has said, we indicate that we understand. Whether we really do or not is immaterial. The point is we have given the speaker the impression that we understand exactly what it is he or she is talking about.

That is not the case with written communication. Here we are not so forgiving. When people write words on paper, we expect them to use the correct words, to say exactly what they mean. That looseness of interpretation goes out the window.

For example, what difference does it make if you say, *You write pretty good*, or *You write very well*.

Bear with us now. The word *pretty* is a descriptive term,

supposedly most often used in the context of *beauty*. The word *good* is usually associated with an evaluation of acceptability. The food is good. The person's behavior is good. The car drives good.

So when you say, *You write pretty good*, the listener can do all kinds of interpreting and come up with an interpretation that is reasonably close to what you intended. But if you write those same words, it comes out, *You write attractive evaluation of acceptability*, or some other equally inane interpretation.

You write very well is only marginally better. But it does come closer to giving your readers the message you want them to receive. But (there's that word again), it can be further improved, tightened, refined, what have you, until you have delivered the message so succinctly that there is no way to misinterpret what you have written. All you have to do is practice.

Practical Practice #5

HERE WE SEARCH TO ELIMINATE VERBOSITY, SESQUIPEDALIANISM, AND WORDINESS. IF THE AUTHORS OF THE FOLLOWING HAD THOUGHT ABOUT WHAT THEY WERE GOING TO WRITE BEFORE THEY STARTED WRITING, THEY WOULD HAVE BEEN MORE CONCISE, CLEAR, AND CONDENSED. WRITE YOUR IMPROVED VERSIONS.

1. The two of us, Kathy and me, sat huddled together, as close as we could possibly be, shivering, knowing that we somehow had to do everything we could possibly do to protect ourselves from the frigid cold of the awesome bone-chilling arctic darkness as it began to close in around us.

2. My brother and me were born just five minutes apart, to the same mother and father, during the same hour, the same day, the same month, and the same year.

3. For the last ninety years, the better part of a whole century, research scientists have continually been searching for the best possible way to develop a cure for the symptoms of the common cold: the sneezes, the sniffles, the hacking cough, and the frequent nose blowing.

4. None of us, and that includes my father as well, had any idea about what we should do when the alien space ship landed in the darkness in our backyard at midnight. Still, my youngest sister, Mary, was the only one who came completely unglued, she ranted and raved and screamed and carried on like a chicken with its head cut off.

5. The tasks were simple. To demonstrate his or her agility, he/ she had to place a single block on top of another single

block. Then he/she had to ride a three-wheeled tricycle.
Then he/she had to pull both ends of a string through a small,
round hole until it was completely through and then he/she
had to walk a singly straight line and he/she had to keep both
feet on it.

6. The five hundred mile race that happens every Memorial Day
in Indianapolis is an annual event that tests both the skill of
the driver and the endurance of the car. During the average
race there will be six caution flags, three wrecks, and one
spectator injury which will cause the overall racing speed of
the race to be diminished.

How did you do? Did you spot the unnecessary words? Did
you eliminate the helpless words that clutter up the sentences?
Did you make the above sentences more reader-friendly?

Helpless Words

Helpless words are words that need modifiers. Helpless words are words that take two or three words to say what one well-chosen word could say.

The best way to spot helpless words is to look for some tag-on modifier that is needed to describe what the writer intended to write.

For instance:

Ran quickly.	Spoke softly.
Smiled happily.	Kissed lightly.
Walked aimlessly.	

See how those words ending in -ly stick out? In each case there is a more precise word that will give your reader a clearer picture of the image you want to convey. In the case of ran quickly, why wouldn't *darted* or *raced* or *bolted* have been more informative and given your reader a clearer picture of what you wanted to say?

Now find the *right* word for the others on the list.

Let us conclude this brief excursion into verbosity, sesquipedalianism, and wordiness with the following advice:

Write Tight and Right Tip

IN GENERAL, THE FEWER WORDS YOU USE IN A SENTENCE, THE GREATER THE IMPACT OF THAT SENTENCE ON A READER. USING LONG, UNGAINLY, AND UNFAMILIAR WORDS WILL DO MORE TO LOSE AND CONFUSE THE READER THAN IMPRESS. WRITE TIGHT.

A Clear and Readable Style: Summary

There are *four kinds of writing*:

Personal —   diaries, journals, feelings, introspective.
Social   —   letters, reports, journalism.
Expressive — expository, academic, extended.
Business —   factual, impersonal, but, above all, brief and concise.

To some extent they overlap.   However, business demands a different kind of writing discipline than the other three types. Brevity and conciseness usually lead to better understanding of what has been written.

The *three cardinal sins of effective business writing* are:

1.   *Verbosity.*
2.   *Sesquipedalianism.*
3.   *Wordiness.*

A *verbose writing style* is one that is flowery or pretentious.

Sesquipedalianism is usually the result when you try to impress your reader with your extensive vocabulary rather than trying to find the precise term to convey your message.

Wordiness is a bad communications habit: The practice of resorting to volumes of words when a few well-chosen ones would accomplish your goal.

Tight Writing Examples

The following exercise will help you understand the concept of tight writing. Study the following sentences. Note how many unnecessary and purposeless words clutter these sentences and keep them from being tightly written.

He was riding a three-wheeled tricycle.
Red blood gushed from the girl's wound.
Ike was strangled to death on the mattress of his bed.

See what's wrong with these? Sure you do. Think about it. *Three-wheeled* and *tricycle* are redundant. In the second sentence, what color is *blood*? In the third sentence, *strangled* and *death* are the same; if you have been *strangled*, you are *dead*. Did you miss one?

Tight writing demands that you strip out the excessive words found in most business correspondence.

He rode a tricycle.
Blood gushed from her wound.
He was strangled in his bed.

Got the concept? Try these. Find the unnecessary words. These may be a little more difficult.
She placed a single block on top of the pile.
We are offering you a very unique opportunity.

In the first sentence, *single* means one. In this sentence, the article *a* means the same. In the second sentence, *unique* means one of a kind. Since it is a unique opportunity, you need not modify it with a word like *very*.

A Wrap-Up To Part One

So, what have we talked about so far? We have talked about how we evolved into what and where we are today. Then we spent some time talking about the necessity to think about what we are going to write before we actually start to write.

After that, we talked about why we write. We decided we write to communicate. Even more importantly, we write because we are moving forward and when we go forward in business that means we are going to have to write more (and better) than we have before.

We spent some time on the components of effective written communication: worthwhile content, readable style, good organization. Every one is essential.

We talked about the principles of reinforcement and of the rules of tight writing. That's when we turned our attention to style. We spent time on the various types of writing, making distinctions about the expectations for each of these styles: personal, social, expressive, and business.

The message is simple. You can improve how well you write in the next few hours. It won't happen automatically. You won't have to master enormous rules of grammar, but you will have to become a believer in the importance of becoming a good communicator.

That's the first step. Now, let's take the second.

Practical Practice #6

DEVELOP THE HABIT OF SEEKING THE RIGHT WORD, A WORD THAT STATES PRECISELY WHAT YOU WANT YOUR READER TO EXPERIENCE. IN AN EARLIER PART OF THIS BOOK , WE PRESENTED THIS EXAMPLE: THE GIRL BEGAN TO CRY.

We went on to point out that by searching for a more precise way of describing how the girl cried, the writer could write the following: The girl began to sob. The girl began to whimper. The girl began to snivel.

Note: Each sentence uses the same number of words. But in each case the selection of a more descriptive and precise word gives the reader more information than the word cry. The new words not only tell the reader what the girl did, but how she did it.

Select suitable synonyms for the following. Try to think of three variations for each.

Example:
appraise   evaluate, calculate, ascertain

beautiful   _____

careless   _____

decent   _____

emotion   _____

fantasize   _____

gloomy   _____

hard   _____

ignorant   _____

joy   _____

kiss   _____

liberty   _____

mad   _____

necessary   _____

opinion   _____

partial   _____

question   _____

refuse   _____

sad   _____

tarnish   _____

unfair   _____

walk   _____

yield   _____

zero   _____

How did you do? Sure it took some doing, but that willingness to search for the right word will make you a more effective communicator on all business correspondence.

Practical Practice #7

TRITE WRITING IS BORING WRITING. TRITE WRITING
IS LAZY WRITING. FIND A FRESH WAY OF
EXPRESSING YOURSELF.

TRITE EXPRESSION	WRITE TIGHT AND RIGHT VERSION
cold sweat	_____
cool as a cucumber	_____
cradle of the deep	_____
crow to pick	_____
daily repast	_____
dead as a doornail	_____
dead giveaway	_____
depths of despair	_____
die is cast	_____
dog days	_____
doomed to disappointment	_____

down my alley _____

draw the line _____

drown one's sorrows _____

fish out of water _____

each and every _____

ear to the ground _____

exception proves the rule _____

eyes of the world _____

face the music _____

fast and loose _____

feather in her cap _____

fill the bill _____

filthy lucre _____

flash in the pan _____

fly off the handle _____

fools rush in   _____

first and foremost   _____

get the upper hand   _____

clear as mud   _____

get what I mean?   _____

gild the lily   _____

grain of salt   _____

Practical Practice #8

A CLEAR AND READABLE STYLE. (SUMMARY SHEET ON PAGE 45.) WE KNOW WHAT WE INTEND TO SAY, BUT OFTEN, IN THE PROCESS OF PUTTING WORDS TO PAPER, OUR WRITING STYLE (THE WAY WE EXPRESS OURSELVES) BECOMES MUDDY AND CONFUSING. HOW WOULD YOU CLEAN UP THE FOLLOWING SENTENCES TO MAKE THEM CLEAR AND READABLE? IF YOU ARE NOT QUITE CERTAIN YOU KNOW HOW TO IMPROVE THESE SENTENCES, IT WILL HELP TO REREAD THE SECTION ON CLEAR AND READABLE STYLE, PAGES 36-45.

1. We stumbled upon an abandoned campsite early, giving somewhat of an uneasy feeling.

_____

_____

_____

_____

2.　　My report is going to cover the most traumatic event of my life, which is something I hope nobody will ever have to go through.

_____

_____

_____

_____

3.　　I inquired as to whom was calling me at work and the reply was my father.

_____

_____

_____

_____

4.   The three of us that were in the out-of-control car were yelling and praying that we would not hit the tree that we were heading directly for.

_____

_____

_____

_____

5.   Both cars were totaled out completely but luckily no real serious injuries occurred to me or nobody else in the other car.

_____

_____

_____

_____

PART II

THE MECHANICS OF WRITING

So much for an overview of business writing. Now you have an idea of the theory behind *Write Tight and Right*. Because many of you may be thinking about the mechanics of grammar and writing for the first time in a long time, a brief refresher would seem to be in order.

A Quick Refresher In Business Writing Mechanics

ABBREVIATIONS: Do not use abbreviations or contractions in formal business writing. It is also good practice to avoid using them in your informal business writing as well.

APOSTROPHE: Use an apostrophe to indicate that a noun is possessive: *Matt's hat. Dr. Seuss's books are good.* For nouns that end in "s" you can choose between either style. *Clemens' penname was Mark Twain* or *Clemens's penname was Mark Twain.*

ARABIC NUMERALS: Use Arabic numerals (0,1,2,3) in measurements, times, numbers, money, and percentages. A rule of thumb is never spell out numerals over ten. Another is never combine spelled out numerals and Arabic numerals.

You could write *"one response,"* or *"1 response"* but never *"one to 15 responses."*

CAPITALIZATION: Capitalize trade names (*Kleenex*), proper nouns (*Ohio River, Lou Holtz*), and nouns used before letters or numerals (*Company C* or *Table A*). Capitalize the first word of a quotation. There is a tendency in business writing to capitalize all titles even when they do not precede a name (*Our Vice President denied the request.*) Don't do it unless policy demands it.

CORRECTIONS: As a general rule, if you have to make a correction you should always retype your document. *Never* strike over an incorrect letter. *Never* make handwritten notes on a typed page of formal or finished correspondence.

DEFINITIONS: If you find it necessary to define a term or procedure, use parentheses without intervening punctuation. She had been a member of the CIA (*Central Intelligence Agency*) for years.

ET CETERA: In business writing, it is good practice to avoid the use of *et cetera, etc., so forth,* and *on and on.* These are terms which imply vague or inexact definition.

FOREIGN TERMS: Always <u>underline</u> or *italicize* foreign words used in business correspondence.

MARGINS: Unless otherwise indicated by corporate practice or culture, make certain all correspondence has a one-inch margin on the top, bottom, and sides of the page.

NAMES: The first time you use a person's or company's name in business correspondence, use the entire name. Example: *Arvin Industries, Joseph Baxter.* Thereafter, in the same piece of correspondence, you may use a shortened reference such as *Arvin* or *Baxter.*

NUMBERING: For short lists, use parenthetical numbers and linear construction. Example: *She handled small animals only: (1) dogs, (2) cats,*

(3) frogs, (4) mice. For longer lists with substantially more data, omit the parentheses and arrange the data in tabular form.
1. *Big dogs with big teeth.*
2. *Big dogs with small teeth.*
3. *Big dogs with false teeth.*

PUNCTUATION:

You should be familiar with basic punctuation.

COMMA:

The comma was invented to help readers. Without commas it is easy to misread sentences. *"If I cook you do the dishes."* or *"If I cook, you do the dishes."* Use a comma if it makes what you have written clearer to the reader or at natural breaks.

COLON:

The primary role of the colon is to call attention to the words that follow it. *The following are tools of writing: paper, word processor, writing books.*

SEMICOLON:

The semicolon is used to connect major sentence elements. The semicolon calls for a voice pause as long as a period, but it is used *only* as internal punctuation.

Some inmates were strung out; others were at peace. Good rule of thumb: Don't use them. Put in a period.

QUOTATION MARKS: Use quotation marks to enclose direct quotations. Bob said, *"Get in, sit down, be quiet."* Do not use quotation marks around indirect quotes. *Bob wondered if he should tell them to get in, sit down and be quiet.* Use single quotation marks to enclose a quotation within a quotation. "Jay, remember what Franklin said, 'Look before you leap.'" (Incidentally, this is the only place single quotation marks are used.) Quotation marks, both double and single, always follow periods and commas. No exceptions.

QUESTION MARKS: Use a question mark after a direct question. *How fast can a horse run?* Do not use a question mark after an indirect question. *I wonder how fast a horse can run.*

EXCLAMATION POINTS: Use an exclamation point when you wish to express exceptional feeling or to give a statement special emphasis. *"He's dead!"* Do not overuse exclamation points.

DASHES:

Dashes are formed with two hyphen marks although you can make a dash on most terminals. The dash is used when, for emphasis, the writer wants a pause longer than a comma calls for or when other commas in the sentence make dashes necessary for clarity. Note: Dashes are greatly overused and most of the time are unnecessary.

SPACING:

Spacing after punctuation. Zero spaces before or after periods in abbreviations (*a.k.a., a.m., etc.*). Zero spaces before or after a hyphen (*self-governing*). One space after commas, semicolons, and colons. One space between initials of a person's name (*J. G. Smith*). Two spaces after punctuation at the end of a sentence.

TITLES:

Underline or italicize the names of aircraft, ballets, books, plays, films, magazines, newspapers, novels, operas, paintings, symphonies, ships, recordings, radio and tv shows. Use quotation marks for short stories, short poems, one-act plays, essays, chapter titles, and other literary works of less than book length.

AND SOME EXTRAS: On occasion it is all right to underline a word to give it emphasis.

Periods and commas are always put inside the quotation marks even when they are not part of the quote. Example*: "Although our minister says 'The way of the transgressor is hard,' I notice our local criminals have an easy time of it."*

Other punctuation marks are put inside of the quotation marks when they are part of the quote and outside when they are not part of the quote. Example: *Cheryl was sobbing, "Why am I so lonely?" Franklin said, "He who hesitates is lost"; he also said, "Look before you leap."*

SLANG: Don't use slang — no matter how "cool" you are.

PROFANITY: If you use profanity, there had better be a damn good reason.

Sentences

First of all, do you still remember that classic definition of a sentence that you were taught when you were a child?

A sentence is a word or group of words which states, asks, commands, or exclaims something.

Oh yeah, you're saying to yourself, I remember. Let us add a couple of things to that.

1.   A sentence begins with a capital letter.
2.   It ends with some kind of punctuation mark.

In other words, a sentence, written properly, is a whole thing. Nine times out of ten, it will express a complete thought or convey a complete message.

Remember all of that?

Let's continue. Most sentences in English begin with the subject, move to a verb, and continue on to an object.

Tom ate oatmeal.

Tom is the subject. The subject is the person or thing doing whatever is being done in the sentence.

Ate is the verb. The verb is any word expressing an action performed or a state of being experienced by the subject (in this case, Tom).

In the sentence, *Tom ate oatmeal, oatmeal* is the object. It's the noun or noun equivalent which receives the action of the verb.

Now back in the days when you were learning your grammar, and the teacher was convinced that you had the concept of sentence structure down pat, you probably were taught to sprinkle in a few modifiers to keep your writing from being too monotonous. For example, you were taught that if you wanted to modify nouns, *Tom* (the subject) and *oatmeal* (the object), you could use something called an adjective. Remember adjectives?

You've got it. *Adjectives are words that qualify, define, or limit nouns.* In other words, if you sprinkle an adjective or two in front of the word Tom in our sentence, the person reading about Tom will know more about him. For example, *Tall and talented Tom ate oatmeal.* Since the object of our sentence (*oatmeal*) is also a noun, we can use adjectives to modify it as well. Suppose we introduce the words *hot* and *sugared* to describe oatmeal. Now we have a sentence that looks like this:

Tall and talented Tom ate hot, sugared oatmeal.

Okay, so much for adjectives that modify nouns.

Practical Practice #9

EDIT THE FOLLOWING SENTENCES FOLLOWING THE STYLE USED BY THE AUTHORS IN THE PRECEDING PAGES.

1. The 10 a.m. launch, delayed a day by NASA, the National Aeronautics and Space Administration, now had only a 50 - minute weather window.

2. Without falling Bob regained his balance and said 'There's nothing to it.'

3. Out of the corner of his eye Tom saw her walk up the lane; he knew the felled tree was his coup de maitre.

4. I asked him if he knew the solution?

5. Bob asked, "Do you know who said "a penny earned is a penny saved?""

6. If I had earned my MBA as our Vice President did, I wouldn't have been in this job for twelve years.

7. The Johnsons house was for sale!

8. I'm sure you know Tyler, our Director of off - shore properties.

9. We had 3 chances —

   1. Sell.

   2. Wait.

   3. Buy more.

10. Can this self tightening lock nut be ordered.

11. It was, you know, the easier course.

12. He asked if I could get tickets for the knock'em-dead show "Phantom of the Opera"?

13. A. G. Smith — my cousin — asked two questions?

14. You know the form; keep talking, et cetera.

15. "If once you fail, try, try again" is a good quote for our use, I said to the Superintendent.

Now, let's look at the words that modify verbs.
The words that modify verbs are called adverbs.
Adverbs can modify or limit verbs, adjectives, or other
adverbs. Just for the heck of it, let's throw a couple of adverbs
into the saga of Tom and his oatmeal.

Tall and talented Tom quickly ate hot, sugared oatmeal.

Yuck. As a written statement designed to convey
information it works. However, it is clumsy, wordy, and lacks
style.

If you were writing about Tom in your diary, *Tom ate
oatmeal* might be sufficient. After all, it might conjure up the
image you were trying to capture. This is called *personal
writing*.

If you were writing about Tom and his oatmeal for your
doctor, attempting to describe his poor eating habits, you might
write *picked at his oatmeal.* This is called *social writing*.

If you were describing how Tom ate that blasted bowl of
hot oats for your college grammar class, you would elaborate
still further and perhaps pile on a few more adjectives and
adverbs (hopefully in a far more effective fashion than we did in
our earlier example) to give the sentence flavor. (Sorry. We
couldn't resist.) This is called *expressive writing*.

But since this whole drill pertains to effective business
writing and not college grammar or a composition class, you
would forego 90 percent of the descriptive add-ons and simply
convey the facts.

What do you know? We're back to *Tom ate oatmeal.* This is *business writing.*

This whole sentence evolution drill is presented here for a purpose. As a concept, particularly for those who have endured numerous high school and/or college level composition courses, the concept of *Write Tight and Right* may come as a bit of learning shock.

In a real sense, business writing tugs in opposition to much that you may have been taught in your expository writing classes. Business writing embraces a writing style that thrives on brevity, conciseness, economy, thoroughness, and preciseness. The driving forces in this communication style are time and accuracy.

Keeping all this in mind, *Tom ate oatmeal* doesn't sound choppy or primitive. It sounds timely, informative, and economical.

Just for the record, there are four (4) basic types of sentences, remember?

Recognizing Sentence Types

1. The Simple Sentence.
2. The Compound Sentence.
3. The Complex Sentence.
4. The Compound-Complex Sentence.

Let's briefly review each of them as a refresher.

The Simple Sentence

A simple sentence is composed of a single independent

clause with no dependent clauses. Did you just flashback to every grammar class you've ever had? Relax. It's okay. What we've really said is the information contained in a simple sentence is whole and complete. It is not dependent on the information contained in any other clause. That didn't hurt much, did it? Furthermore, a simple sentence often has one subject and one predicate. But that doesn't mean that the sentence has to sound simple. A simple sentence may contain modifying words or phrases.

Mary Wollstonecraft Shelley wrote <u>Frankenstein</u>.
Her book is a classic and renowned as a study in terror.

Write Tight and Right Tip
SIMPLE SENTENCES SELDOM CONTAIN ANY PUNCTUTATION OTHER THAN THE PUNCTUATION REQUIRED AT THE END OF A SENTENCE: A PERIOD, QUESTION MARK, OR EXCLAMATION POINT.

The Compound Sentence

A compound sentence is composed of two or more independent clauses. In other words, each of these independent clauses contains enough information to be a simple sentence and stand by itself. These clauses usually are connected by a conjunction (*so, yet, nor, or, for, but,* or, *and*). You will use a comma before, not after, the conjunction.

She wrote the book early in her adult life, and her mother was chagrined.

Write Tight and Right Tip

THE COMMA AND CONJUNCTION CONNECT TWO OTHERWISE INDEPENDENT CLAUSES AND MAKE THE SENTENCE COMPOUND.

The Complex Sentence

The complex sentence differs from the compound sentence because it contains one independent clause and one or more dependent clauses. An independent clause contains enough information to stand by itself (a simple sentence), but the dependent clause cannot stand by itself.

Before she became an author, Shelley relied on her husband's income.

The dependent clause starts with *Before*. The independent clause begins with *Shelley*.

Write Tight and Right Tip

WHEN A DEPENDENT CLAUSE COMES BEFORE AN INDEPENDENT CLAUSE, THE CLAUSES ARE USUALLY SEPARATED BY A COMMA.

The Compound-Complex Sentence

A compound-complex sentence joins a compound sentence and a complex sentence. A sentence thus structured contains two or more independent clauses and one or more dependent clauses.

When it became apparent that the fans could no longer afford the tickets, baseball became an electronic game, and it was no longer considered America's pastime.

The dependent clause begins with *When*, the independent clauses start with *baseball*, and with *it*.

So much for our review of the four basic sentence types. If you have been out of school for more than a few years, it was probably worth the brief time it took to review them.

Recognizing Different Kinds of Sentences

We complete our brief review of sentences, their structure, punctuation, and types, by reviewing the uses of sentences. There are four kinds of sentences:
1. Declarative.
2. Imperative.
3. Interrogative.
4. Exclamatory.

Declarative sentences make statements:
Rod Serling wrote <u>The Twilight Zone</u>.

Imperative sentences issue requests or make demands: *Watch <u>The Twilight Zone</u>.*

Interrogative sentences ask questions: *Did you watch <u>The Twilight Zone</u>?*

Exclamatory sentences are statements in which the punctuation at the end of the sentence (*!*) tells the reader the author feels the sentence requires additional emphasis: *<u>The Twilight Zone</u> is a great tv show*!

Write Tight and Right Tip

A PRACTIONER OF THE WRITE TIGHT AND RIGHT CONCEPT WILL SELDOM USE THE COMPOUND-COMPLEX OR EXCLAMATORY SENTENCE STRUCTURES. THE FORMER ARE TOO LONG AND CONVOLUTED FOR BUSINESS WRITING, AND THE LATTER UNNECESSARY WHEN WRITERS CHOOSE CORRECT NOUNS AND VERBS TO CONSTRUCT EFFECTIVE BUSINESS SENTENCES.

Sentences: Summary

A sentence is a word or group of words which state, ask, command, or exclaim something. Sentences start with a capital letter and end with some kind of appropriate punctuation. There are four basic types of sentences:

1. A simple sentence.
2. A compound sentence.
3. A complex sentence.
4. A compound-complex sentence.

There are four basic uses of sentences:

1. Declarative sentences.
2. Imperative sentences.
3. Interrogative sentences.
4. Exclamatory sentences.

Paragraphs

A paragraph is a distinct unit of writing, generally containing more than one sentence. The paragraph is viewed as a document subsection that is devoted to a particular point contained in that document.

A writer begins a new paragraph on a new line to show the reader that there is a shift in the writer's point of view or the direction of the document.

It is customary in business writing to indent each paragraph.

The Nature of Paragraphs

Except for special purpose paragraphs, such as an introductory paragraph or a concluding paragraph in a business document, the basic paragraph is a cluster of information that advances the premise of the document.

A well-constructed paragraph is clearly focused, well developed, tightly written, painstakingly organized, and coherent.

In a well-written business document, the paragraph is neither too long nor too short. The length of paragraphs will vary, if for no other reason than to avoid monotony and repetition in the business document.

Paragraphs Should Be Focused

All paragraphs should be unified around the focal point of the document. This unification is called focus. That focus should be on specific points. The purpose of that focus should be apparent to the reader from the outset. If, after reading the opening sentence of a paragraph, the reader isn't certain where the writer is headed, it's safe to say that the opening sentence should probably be redrafted and reconstructed.

As readers move into a paragraph, they need to know where they are, both in relation to the focus of that particular document and what to expect in the sentences still to come. Think of it this way: The lead sentence in a paragraph in a business memo, letter, or report is like the topic sentence in an essay or the thesis statement in a research paper.

However, that is where the similarity ends. In business writing there is little room (or need) for displays of expressive writing. The need for creativity is still there because tight writing does not come easily for some people. It is altogether possible that learning to *Write Tight and Right* will tax your creative juices far more than you imagined.

> **Write Tight and Right Tip**
> DO NOT STRAY FROM THE
> POINT OF YOUR PARAGRAPH.

Paragraphs Should Be Carefully Developed

Now that you have established what the main point of the paragraph is, you need to develop that point. In other words, now it is up to you to show the reader that you can support your focus sentence. It is not enough just to make the flat statement:

Stephen King is now the most published author of all time.

Now you need to be able to reinforce that assertion with supporting, follow-on information.

Why? Because when you make such sweeping statements, you can fully expect someone to say, "Oh yeah, who says?"

So, after making the assertion that King is the most published author of all time, you follow on with a series of sentences designed to convince the reader that what you say is true. For example, you might write:

King's 1987 release, The Tommyknockers, brings his total number of best sellers to 37.

Then, to further support your contention, you build on the above base sentence by writing:

These novels, combined with King's anthologies, works written under the pseudonym of Richard Bachman, screenplays, and non-fiction works, bring the total number of published works to 54.

Then you may add a sentence that reads something like:

A spokesperson for <u>Publisher's Weekly</u> indicates that King's publisher has just released figures indicating there are now more copies of King's work in print than any other author.

At this point you are well on your way to a well-developed paragraph that looks something like this:

Stephen King is now the most published author of all time. King's 1987 release, <u>The Tommyknockers</u>, brings his total number of best sellers to 37. These novels, combined with King's anthologies, works written under the pseudonym of Richard Bachman, screenplays, and non-fiction works, bring the total number of published works to 54. A spokesperson for <u>Publisher's Weekly</u> indicates that King's publisher has just released figures indicating there are now more copies of King's work in print than any other author.

So what do we have? We have a paragraph that begins with a lead sentence making a statement. The three sentences that follow fall in line to support that lead sentence. At the same time, the author is indicating what is being used to support the contention of the lead sentence, namely facts and figures. Finally, the author reveals the source of that information. If that isn't enough, the author uses numbers to further support and develop the paragraph.

Write Tight and Right Tip
START A PARAGRAPH WITH A BROAD
STATEMENT AND MAKE SUCCEEDING
STATEMENTS IN THAT PARAGRAPH MORE
DEFINITE.

Paragraphs Should Be Tightly Written

Throughout this workbook we dwell on the concept of *Write Tight and Right*. The concept can be best demonstrated in the editing and revision process. Consider the following:

A writer who insists on using long, complicated sentences often does more to confuse his readers than inform them of new information. We firmly believe that a simple sentence, void of unnecessary punctuation, has far more impact, and that it is far more likely that the writer will get the desired response from the reader.

Now take out the unnecessary words that do nothing to

enhance comprehension:

> ~~A writer who insists on using~~ <u>l</u>ong, complicated
>   **do**
> sentences ~~often does~~ more to confuse his readers than inform
> them. ~~of new information.~~ ~~We firmly believe that~~ <u>a</u> simple
> sentence, ~~void of unnecessary punctuation~~, has *far* more
>   **to**
> impact, and ~~that it~~ is *far* more likely ~~that the writer will~~ get the
> desired response from the reader.

What do you have? You have a paragraph with 26 fewer words and just as much information. It is called *tight writing*.

Long, complicated sentences do more to confuse readers than inform them. A simple sentence has more impact and is more likely to get the desired response from the reader.

Write Tight and Right Tip
EDIT. EDIT. EDIT.
EDITING IS THE KEY TO WRITING TIGHT.

Paragraphs Should Be Well Organized

Some people seem to have trouble grasping the concept

of paragraph organization. That problem can be resolved when a way of looking at sequential organization is presented. For example, one suggestion is that it might help if a person would think of a paragraph as a unit in which all the bits of information had shapes.

"When you're clustering information," the person recommended, "try to think of each bit of information as having a shape. Then, put all the circles in one paragraph, the straight lines in another, the horseshoe shaped items in another, and so on."

Another cautioned, "Don't put red facts in a blue paragraph. Put red facts in a paragraph about red things. Put blue facts in a paragraph about blue things. If you run across something green, it may mean you'll have to develop a green paragraph."

Put another way, one writer said, "An organized paragraph is a readable paragraph. There is a logical sequence in the way the paragraph reads and progresses."

From still another perspective, "The ideal paragraph is constructed in much the same way as a good set of directions on how to get from point A to point B are fashioned. First you ease the person into the situation from a common starting point. Then you give clear instructions referencing landmarks or identifiable benchmarks until the directions narrow in on the destination (conclusion)."

Paragraphs Should Be Coherent

Finally, there is the matter of coherency.

By that we mean consistent throughout.

In the final analysis, in order for a paragraph to be consistent throughout, the author should:

1. Avoid abrupt changes in style.
2. Keep the content focused.
3. Try to deliver the information at the same pace and with the same degree of thoroughness.
4. Use transitions. They are like roadsigns for the reader. Transitions help guide the reader through both the paragraph and the document.

Coherency encompasses all these things. Of all the cautions we must guard against in our writing, coherency may be the easiest to let slip away.

Why?

Because the other elements of writing — keeping focused, systematic development, tight writing, and careful organization — are learned or mechanical. They are skill related, and the more we do them, the more likely we are to become proficient. That is not the case with coherency or consistency.

By the same token, we must always guard against choppy writing. At the same time, we must avoid writing up or down to our audience. We must remember that effective writing, in addition to all of the above, must be readable.

Finally, A Potpourri of Paragraph Paradigms

So, exactly when do you break off from one paragraph

and start another?

It may surprise you to learn that the breaks between paragraphs are not always made for 100 percent logical reasons. In addition to all the reasons we have listed, a writer may use a paragraph break to indicate a shift in emphasis, a different time, a different place, contrast, breaking up a page that looks too dense, and giving the reader a break.

It is in page construction (and you do that with paragraphs) that you really do go from grammar machine to writer.

Finally, after preaching the gospel of writing tight for so many pages, a word of reverse caution. Beware of using too many short sentences in short paragraphs. Even business readers want reading material that flows, seeing ideas that link, and being comfortable with what they are reading.

There are times, occasionally, when it makes sense to combine paragraphs. If combining paragraphs enhances the document's organization, do it. If combining paragraphs will enhance the document's impact and increase the likelihood of getting your message across, do it.

Write Tight and Right Tip
IF YOU THINK IT WILL GIVE YOUR READERS A CLEARER SENSE OF UNDERSTANDING OF THE DOCUMENT'S CONTENT, DO IT.

Paragraphs: Summary

A well-constructed paragraph is:

1. Clearly focused.
2. Well developed.
3. Tightly written.
4. Painstakingly organized.
5. Coherent.

Clearly focused:	Unified around a central theme.
Well developed:	You can support what you write.
Tightly written:	Your writing has been revised and edited.
Painstakingly organized:	A logical, progressive sequence.
Coherent:	Your structure and writing should be consistent.

Paragraph breaks are used to:

1. Indicate a shift in emphasis.
2. Indicate different time.
3. Indicate different place.
4. Demonstrate contrast.
5. Break up a dense page.
6. Give the reader a break.

On occasion a paragraph can be lengthened if it:

1. Enhances the document's impact.
2. Increases the likelihood of conveying your message.

Practical Practice #10

USE A MARK TO INDICATE WHERE YOU
WOULD MAKE PARAGRAPH DIVISIONS IN THE
LONGER PARAGRAPH BELOW. ALSO WRITE WHY
YOU BELIEVE THESE DIVISIONS ARE APPROPRIATE.

The company has one month to finish the proposal.
This period should allow sufficient time for all personnel to
participate and evaluate the proposal before it is sent. If the
original draft is completed in the customary two months, we
still have a week for revisions and another for final evaluation.
The officers have decided upon the following proposal draft
plan. The proposal will be drafted by the San Francisco office.
Revisions will be made by the New York City office. The final
evaluation will be handled by the Chicago headquarters. San
Francisco Vice President John Haller will be in charge of the
draft team. All personnel in the San Francisco office will be
notified by their supervisors that they are to check with them
daily. Any reassignments needed will be determined by Haller.
He will report daily progress to both the main office and to the
New York City office. The revision team will be led by New
York City Vice President Sandra Lolich. As was the case in
San Francisco, all personnel will be notified to check with their
supervisors daily. Lolich will file daily progress reports with the
main office. When the revision team has completed its work,
the final evaluation team will be composed of Haller, Lolich,
and President Tim Merritt. They will make any decisions in
compromising the draft and the revision. President Merritt will
decide how this final evaluation process will take place, either
by e-mail, telephone, or conference at the Chicago

headquarters. In the meantime, the cooperation of all personnel in completing this project is appreciated. It is obvious that it is critical to the growth of the company. Your hard work is necessary and valued!

Reasons for you paragraph divisions:

Editing and Revision

Not long ago, a young man came up after one of our writing seminars. He looked distraught. "I hear what you're saying about editing and revision," he said. "But I don't have the slightest idea how to go about it. How do you edit?"

After thinking about it for a moment, we explained how we edited our own material. That evening, we riffled back through our editorial notes to *Write Tight and Right* which still were in first draft stage.

It seemed to us the young man was correct. We had been drumming away on the subject of *Tight Writing* — of which editing and revision are two major components — for nearly seven and a half hours in a day-long seminar without explaining how to go about the process.

The following should correct that oversight.

Let us start with the fact that both authors are avid proponents of the *get it on paper* school of writing. In other words, we believe that when you start to author a document (memo, poem, love letter, letter to the editor, financial report, research document, essay, business letter, etc.) you should get the words on paper just as fast as possible.

Let the words flow. Let the idea crystallize. Don't take time to go back and cross t's, don't dot i's, don't correct spelling, don't question your punctuation. Just get the whole message down where you can see if you really have a legitimate opening, a message, and a close.

Why?

Because if you go back and start fixing things before the whole idea has a chance to blossom, you start to lose some of the salient reasons for authoring the document in the first place even if you are working from an outline.

In order to demonstrate effective editing and revision, let's say you have hammered out the first draft of your document. In other words, it's on paper. But it doesn't look like much. Now, what do you do?

You start by reading what you have written. During this first peek at what's on paper, you look for opportunities to add meat to your document. This is where you sprinkle your text with facts and details. Also on this first review, you look for places where you repeated yourself or where what you wrote does nothing to advance the purpose of your document. When you find these flaws, fix them.

On a second pass, clarify what needs to be clarified and delete what needs to be deleted. At this point, you will begin to identify the words that just don't belong there. Change them. Get rid of them. Find better words.

By now, your document is taking shape and you'll know if some particular word, sentence, or paragraph supports or detracts from your document. By the way, while you're at it, try to determine if moving a particular block of text — maybe a whole paragraph — will improve the flow of your message.

On the third edit, clean up grammar, spelling, jargon, slang, and sexist language. In other words, search for language more (if not most) appropriate to your purpose.

While you are reviewing, keep in mind that the only way to become truly proficient in your business writing is to put these principles into practice, again, and again, and again.

It also helps if your last edit can be delayed until the next day. Of course, you may not have this luxury. But it's amazing what you can see the next day that you didn't the day before. So, if possible, *always* final edit the next day.

Editing and Revision: Summary

CHECKLIST:

1. Do you have enough facts, details, examples?
2. Have you deleted repetitious, ineffective, inappropriate text?
3. Is your document strong enough to accomplish your goals?
4. What needs to be clarified?
5. How can you strengthen the words?
6. Is your document well organized? Should text be rearranged?
7. Is the language appropriate for audience, objective, and subject matter?
8. Have you edited and revised, if possible delaying the last edit a day?

Learning to Edit: Examples

Definition of edit: *To alter material for publication to make it suitable for one's purpose.*

Definition of revision: *To reexamine in order to discover and amend errors in a text.*

Let's see how much you know about editing or revision. Reduce the number of words in the following sentence without depriving the reader of information.

Robert Miller was a soft-spoken professor who frowned repeatedly when he was describing the assassination of President John Fitzgerald Kennedy that fateful day in Dallas, Texas.

Examine the above sentence, line by line, word by word. How many words can be deleted without compromising the integrity of the information? Several people have successfully reduced the above to 12 words. (Try *Soft-spoken Professor Robert Miller frowned repeatedly when describing President Kennedy's assassination.*) This is what *tight writing* is all about.

But the process of editing or revision is not just a routine whereby we remove verbiage.

Often, we can improve a document by simply changing one word. In some cases, the communication is edited by looking for places where altering one specific word can give the reader more information than the original.

Here's an example: *He walked slowly to the park to meet his contact.*

Start with the phrase *walked slowly*. Reduce it to one word which gives the reader a picture of how the man walked. How about *trudged, plodded*, or *ambled*? Maybe he *waddled, wobbled*, or *shuffled*.

See what you've done? You have reduced the number of words in your document by only one word. But by using a specific word to describe how the man walked, you are giving your reader more information. One thing for certain: There are more precise words than *walk*.

Just for the fun of it, think of other words that might describe how the man walked to the park. Some of them might sound contrived, but nevertheless you can see how words like *strode, proceeded, hiked, tramped*, or *marched* make your writing more alive, more exact, and certainly more interesting.

Try this one: *She cried.*

But how did she cry? *Softly? Hard? Long? Briefly?*

Any one of the following would give the reader more information: *Wept, bawled, blubbered, whimpered, whined, sniveled, moaned, wailed, groaned, lamented.* Want more? *Bewailed, squalled, bellowed, screamed, shrieked.*

Hey, we're not talking about replacing 10-cent words with 50-cent words. Nor are we talking about some esoteric vocabulary learning exercise that consists primarily of six-syllable words. We simply are talking about trying to think of everyday words that more clearly paint a word picture of what you want to say. In most cases, these are words that are part of your vocabulary. You just aren't in the habit of using them.

Just in case you still don't have the hang of it, try this one. Consider the woman who files harassment charges against her employer and says, "He touched me."

Did he brush her shoulder as he passed her chair? Or, was his contact decidedly more intimate? Instead of *touch*, perhaps she should have said *felt, fingered, caressed, fondled, pawed, petted, pressed.* These words bring the gravity of her complaint more clearly into focus than *touched.*

The same exercise applies to finding the noun that best serves your communication purpose.

Suppose you write: *Sharon ate breakfast.* Now, what do you know? Well, you know that Sharon ate breakfast. Nothing more. But suppose you told us: *Sharon ate cereal.* All you did was change one word. The sentence isn't any longer. It's still just three words, but the reader now knows more. All because the communicator took time to look for a more precise word.

But suppose you told us: *Sharon ate oatmeal.* Son-of-a-gun. Still three words, but we know even more. Now we know what kind of cereal.

This simple little drill — the act of getting an individual to search for the right word, the word that will give the reader more information — is one of the most difficult changes to make in the way people think about written communication. It is the basic reason why 9 out of 10 business people believe they need to improve their written communication skills.

Write Tight and Right Tip

REVISING AND EDITING ARE VITAL TO EFFECTIVE WRITTEN COMMUNICATION. EVEN WHEN YOU HAVE GIVEN A GREAT DEAL OF THOUGHT TO THE DOCUMENT'S CONTENT, YOU WILL DISCOVER THAT AS MANY AS TEN PERCENT OF THE WORDS USED SERVE NO PURPOSE AND DO NOTHING TO ENHANCE READABILITY.

Wordiness and Editing: Summary

Wordiness is best personified in the use of *empty* words and *helpless* words.

Empty words are used to modify words that cannot be modified. For example, there is no such thing as *almost impossible.* It either is, or it isn't. If it isn't, it is not *almost impossible*, it is very difficult.

Helpless words are words that must be propped up with modifiers in order to be effective: running quickly, breathed deeply. The former should be *sprinted* or *dashed.* The latter would be stronger as *gasped* or *gulped air.*

Editing is a learned skill. You edit when you take out unnecessary words (wordiness, empty words, helpless words) and try to tighten your writing by focusing on desirable written communication qualities such as brevity, conciseness, and preciseness.

Revision, like editing, is a learned skill. It differs from editing by emphasizing the importance of looking for the word or words that will give the reader a clearer understanding of the written text.

Tight Writing Drill

Many people have difficulty with sentence clarity because of the way they construct their sentences. In many cases they are uncertain where one sentence ends and the next one begins. Because of this uncertainty, they sometimes break what could be a compound sentence into two parts, using a period where they could use a comma or semicolon. In many cases, the result is two short sentences that could be combined into one sentence. Example:

1. *Kevin met George on a train several years ago. He was coming home from the convention.* (Choppy?)

2. *Kevin met George on a train several years ago;*

he was coming home from the convention.
(Unified.)

Note: In the example above, the period was replaced by a semicolon, forming a compound sentence. That same sentence could be further tightened by writing:

3.   *Kevin met George years ago on the train from the convention.*

Now, note what we have done. In the #2 example we have a 16-word sentence. It is correct, but in #3 we have a *write tight* version. It says the same thing but in five fewer words.

Whenever you are constructing any kind of text intended for business communication purposes, keep in mind that you want to make your text as clear as possible and you want to write it with as few words as possible. Both objectives will help you achieve your goal of writing *tight and right.*

The Art of Using Plain English

No discussion of editing and revision would be complete without a section on what we like to call "taking out the garbage."

Taking out the garbage consists in getting rid of those little gems that creep into our writing without us knowing why they are there in the first place.

Chief among these letter-writing sins are *letterese* and *jargon* and *slang.*

Let's start with *letterese.*

Letterese is a malady that strikes perfectly sane people when they quit talking and pick up a pen. Suddenly, those two- and three-syllable words these folks normally use become four- and five- syllable words. They start spewing out tongue twisters such as "At this time I wish to express my deepest gratitude," when they mean to say, "Thank you."

What's wrong with this, you ask? To start with, they are overblown, overused, exaggerated, wordy. If that isn't enough, they sound insincere. Ninety-nine out of one hundred business people will tell you they don't have either the time or patience to read documents containing that kind of garbage.

First we'll deal with letterese. Here is a list of just some of the old saws that poor writers lapse into when they pick up a pen to write.

Old-Fashioned Way	**'90's Way**
at the present time	now
I beg to differ	I disagree
I am cognizant of the fact	I know
Enclosed you will find	Enclosed (Attached)
In accordance with your request	As requested
Please be advised that	Be advised

We acknowledge receipt of	We received
In this day and age	Today
We are aware of the fact	We know
A large number of	Many
The majority of	Most
Due to the fact that	Because
Readily apparant	Obvious
Prior to	Before

These are the same writers who feel compelled to lapse into redundancy to impress the reader with the seriousness of their message.

They do this by sticking to the *basic* essentials, by working toward *mutual* cooperation, by achieving an *end* result, by having a *consensus* of opinion, by striving for the *utmost* perfection, and always considering their *fellow* colleagues. It is these hidden redundancies that trip up many writers. If you aren't absolutely sure how a word should be used, look it up.

When we say get the garbage out of your writing, we are talking about avoiding needless words and phrases. You can learn to write better business letters by using fewer words.

PRACTICAL PRACTICE #11

GETTING RID OF LETTERESE OR AS WE SAY, "TAKING OUT THE GARBAGE." SOME FOLKS TAKE ON A JEKYLL AND HYDE PERSONALITY WHEN THEY SIT DOWN TO WRITE. THE MOMENT THEY PICK UP A PEN, THEY BEGIN TO SEARCH FOR LARGER AND MORE COMPLICATED WORDS THAN THEY WOULD USE IN THEIR DAY-TO-DAY CONVERSATION. THEREFORE, WHAT THEY WRITE SOUNDS AFFECTED AND PRETENTIOUS. WRITE WHAT YOU MEAN, NOT WHAT AND HOW YOU THINK A BUSINESS LETTER IS SUPPOSED TO SOUND.

LETTERESE	WRITE TIGHT AND RIGHT VERSION
Please do not hesitate to call	_____
Pursuant to our agreement	_____
Reached the conclusion	_____
Seldom if ever	_____
Please sign on the designated line	_____
This is to inform you that	_____
Until such time as	_____
We ask your kind permission	_____

The Mechanics of Writing

We wish to acknowledge _____

We would like to ask _____

Will be kind enough _____

Despite the fact that _____

Due to the fact that _____

In this day and age _____

Kindly be advised _____

In the near future _____

In the event that _____

A large number of _____

It is circular in shape _____

At the present lime _____

At a later date _____

Are of the opinion that _____

At all times _____

Attached please find _____

Made the announcement that _____

Numbers, Units, and Other Technical Stuff

Several years ago, E. L. Byer, then director of engineering for ITT-Aerospace, was talking to one of his technical managers. The manager insisted he had communicated "precisely" and "exactly" the instructions for calibrating a certain piece of lab equipment.

"Did you use words or numbers in instructing the man?" Byer thundered.

"Words," the lab manager finally admitted.

"Then you weren't very precise," Byer growled. "Words are not precise. Numbers are precise."

Unfortunately, Mr. Byer is correct. Words mean whatever we have been taught that they mean. Words are imprecise. If you want proof, ask 50 different people what they believe the word nice means. You will probably get at least 35 different definitions with 10 members of your group telling you that nice means good. Now ask them what good means.

Moral: There are times when you simply have to communicate with numbers. Since few people do it well, you need to learn to correctly communicate with numbers.

Let's start with the two main types of business communication that most frequently lean on numbers, units, and other technical symbols:

1. The financial report.
2. The technical or engineering report.

There are more. For our purposes, they are all one and the same, but only because they each use numbers. The financial report uses its own format to convey financial information. You'll find page after page of this kind of information in every annual report, prospectus, financial analysis, etc. These formatted figures are easy to understand. After all, they are arranged in neat columns. The problem is that all too many people forget it is often necessary to comment on those financial exhibits, and, when we do, it has to be done in acceptable, accurate, and – here's the key word — consistent manner. Why? So that people will understand.

Let's say you just purchased a Formula One race car. It weighs *three-quarters of a ton* or *1500 pounds.* Which is correct? Both? What if we said it weighed *3/4 of a ton?* Is that the same as *1500 pounds?* Or should that be *1,500 pounds* with a comma between the *1* and the *5?* Should it be *0.75* or *.75?*

So, we are passing along the general rules that are the most universally accepted, and the rules that most business people tell us they apply in their day-to-day communications efforts.

Let's Talk Numbers

1. Write out all numbers below 10 except when those numbers are used with time (dates), page numbers, money, measures, and percentages:

a. *5 inches,* b. *8 years old,* c. *Page 3,* d. *5 p.m.,* e. *9 percent*

2. A number above nine is usually written in numerals:

> *Pete Rose had more than 4,000 base hits.*
> *The population exceeds 250,000,000 people.*

3. Numbers in the thousands should be written with a

comma:

> a.　　*1500* should be written *1,500*

4. Numbers in the millions can be written either:

> a.　　*75,000,000,*　b.　　*75 million*

5. Numbers above the million mark should not be written using the words trillion, quadrillion, and whatever comes after that because there is too much confusion about what these words actually mean. By the same token, scientific notation methods are equally unfamiliar to most readers. So the best method, even though you have one of those mind-bending numbers, is to print it all out:

> *567,000,000,000,000,000,000 paper clips*

6. Decimals and fractions are always written as numerals:

> a.　　*Zero-point-four-five is 0.45.*
> b.　　*Three-fifths or 3/5 is 0.6.*

7. Use numerals whenever possible.

8. Whenever a number is an approximation, write it out. Use *hedge* words or phrases such as *almost, more or less, roughly*, or *approximately* to tell the reader that these numbers

are not precise measurements:

a. *About 1/2 mile down the road* should be *About one-half mile down the road.*

b. *He drank a little more than 2 beers* should read *He drank a little more than two beers.*

9. Never begin a sentence with a numeral. If you have to use a number to begin a sentence, spell it out:

a. *75,000 people attended the game* should read *Seventy-five thousand people attended the game.*

Let's Talk Units of Measure

1. Units of measure must be consistent throughout the text. Before you start to write your document, determine which system of units you will use. Will it be English? Will it be metric? If your reader (audience) is primarily American, and you are more comfortable with the English Unit, use it. If your document is being prepared for more of an international audience, better consider using metric. Incidentally, there are two metric systems, the cgs Unit and the SI (Systeme International) Unit. SI is more widely used.

2. Write units of measure as words or symbols. Don't abbreviate. The best way to handle this is to let common sense be your guide. Do what you have to do to make certain the material is clear to your reader.

Something To Talk About

It is generally true that numbers, symbols, units of measurement, equations, and other scientific or technical stuff tend to make your readers a bit nervous. Even if your readers are technically minded, the people who type your letters, print your books, or follow your instructions may not be, and all those brackets, arrows, mathematical symbols, and such become opportunities for errors in editing and misunderstanding.

If you must include something like an equation or a formula, center it on a line by itself in the middle of the page.

Finally, define the symbols you use in your document. Don't make your reader guess what you mean when you use an ^ or an |; spell it out.

Write Tight and Right Tip

GOOD TECHNICAL WRITING IS ACCURATE, CLEAR (GRAMMAR, SPELLING, PUNCTUA-TION), CONCISE (FOCUSED), READABLE (INTERESTING), AND CONSISTENT. JUST BECAUSE IT'S TECHNICAL IN NATURE, DOESN'T MEAN IT HAS TO BE BORING.

Practical Practice #12

PAGES 99-103 DEAL WITH WRITING ABOUT
NUMBERS, UNITS, AND OTHER TECHNICAL STUFF.
WHAT DO YOU REMEMBER FROM THAT SECTION?
TAKE A QUICK EXCURSION THROUGH THE
FOLLOWING QUESTIONS AND EVALUATE YOUR
PROGRESS.

1. Numbers below 10 are written out except for what five
exceptions?

_____, _____, _____, _____, _____.

2. A number above nine is always written in numerals.
True or false?

3. Is there more than one way to write or record numbers
in the millions? If so, give examples:

_____.

4. Use the correct form of a number defining trillion,
quadrillion, and septillion.

_____, _____, _____.

5. Are decimals and fractions best expressed in words or
numerals? Give an example:

_____.

6. Circle the correct form for use in a business letter.
(a) three-fifths   (b) 3/5   (c) 0.6

7.   What is the writing rule when a number is an
     approximation?

_____.

8.   Which is correct?
     (a) I leave a little past 2:00 every day.
     (b) I leave a little past two every day.

9.   What is the rule if a sentence begins with a number?

_____.

10. Units of measure can be expressed as either words or
     symbols. True or false?

11. There are three different metric systems and in America
     we use the GB metric system. True or false?

12. It is perfectly acceptable to use technical abbreviations
     in business writing. True or false?

13. Symbols used in technical writing should be defined in a
     special section of the letter or report devoted to
     clarification of terminology. True or false?

GO BACK TO THE NUMBERS SECTION TO SEE HOW
YOU DID.

Our Top 10 Rules For Solving Grammar and Punctuation Problems

These rules won't solve every problem. But from considerable experience, we can assure you that if you use them to question and edit your writing, you will eliminate the vast amount of your grammar and punctuation errors.

RULE #1. The comma and the period always precede the closing quotation marks. There are no exceptions. Yes, we know you see it done the other way, maybe even most of the time. Every time it's done, it's an error. *There are no exceptions.* Example: *She looked at the report and immediately pronounced it to be "quaint."*

RULE #2. Determine whether the style you are using has a comma before the final connector in a series, usually the word *and.* The style of this workbook uses the comma. Some other styles do not. Look through your writing for any series and edit accordingly. Example: *He was hot, ill, and angry.*

RULE #3. Do *not* use a comma when connecting two verbs which have a single subject. (You need to examine a sentence carefully to determine what are the subjects and verbs.) Example: *Chris took the knife in his left hand and held the loaf of bread in his right.* No comma before *and held.* This sentence has a single subject, *Chris*, and two verbs, *took* and *held*, joined by *and.*

RULE #4. You are always on safer ground for two reasons to use few if any semicolons or other ways to connect two sentences. First, it's easy to make an error and, second, it's easier to read short sentences. Example: *Sales on Tuesday reached a high for the decade. Immediately, these figures were* *reflected in increased activity in stock market trading.* That's easier to read than the following: *Sales on Tuesday reached a high for the decade, and immediately these figures were reflected in increased activity in stock market trading.*

RULE #5. If you're never certain about *to, too,* and *two* or *principal/principle* or *capital/capitol* or similar words, use the dictionary. We've been writing for decades and we use the dictionary every day. It's a mark of arrogance to disdain it.

RULE #6. The greatest sin in business writing is overcapitalization, particularly so-called false titles or capitalization where grammatically it is incorrect. Corporate culture may make it something over which you have no control, of course. Example: *The Comptroller announced a Stock Dividend to be shared by all Employees.* That's incorrect. Every capital letter in this sentence should go.

RULE #7. Pronouns need to be in agreement with the words they represent. Sometimes it's difficult to know what word the pronoun has replaced. Example: *The company's issue, one of thousands traded on the world's stock exchanges, was perceived by most buyers to have lost its drive.* The proper pronoun is *its* because the antecedent — way back there — is *issue.* Because it is so easy to make a mistake, our advice is this: Find every pronoun in your writing and its antecedent. Make certain they agree, singular with singular, plural with plural. Yes, it will take time. But the more you do it, the easier and faster the practice will become. Believe us, the grammarians among your readers will notice the difference.

RULE #8. Naturally, subjects and verbs also need to be in agreement, singular with singular and plural with plural. If you learned to diagram sentences — the greatest single grammatical aid that exists — then you won't have any trouble.

If not, it's going to take some effort. Example: *The rate of accidents is increasing.* *Rate* is the subject, not *accidents*, which is the object of the preposition *of*.

RULE #9. With very few exceptions, only put end punctuation, such as a period, at the end of a sentence. Today, much advertising and writing treats phrases as sentences. We've done it a few times in this workbook. When we have, we've done it for emphasis and to have a lighter spirit in places. Generally speaking, though, don't do it. Grammatically, it is *never* correct. Example: *He was satisfied. At least for awhile.* The second period does not follow a sentence, *At least for awhile.* It is a phrase with no subject and no verb.

RULE #10. The best advice of all? Keep your sentences short. Nothing reduces the chance for error as much as short, and for the most part simple, sentences.

Part III

Internal Documents

Before We Begin, A Couple of Distinctions

For years, we have noticed that many text books designed for writing courses, particularly text books designed to teach business writing, make a strange, and to us at least, and erroneous distinction.

For example, many authors of business writing texts categorize one type of letter writing drill as learning to write a *good news* type of correspondence and another as learning to write *unfavorable* or *bad news*.

From there, they frequently meander into a morass of even stranger categories with no clear lines of audience or purpose distinction, often wandering even farther into areas where writing styles are generally dictated by corporate culture, not academic delineation or categorizing.

The fact of the matter is that the most obvious distinction in business writing in the 90's has nothing to do with the nature of the news. It has to do with the correspondence destination. The more appropriate question and by far the most important distinction is whether the document is an *internal document* or an *external document*.

If the primary consideration in all writing is the *audience* or *reader*, there is no bigger distinction than whether or not the person reading your document is inside or outside your company.

When you communicate with individuals or groups of individuals *inside* your company, you are dealing with people who know (or should know) more about your company and its problems, cultures, patterns, and opportunities than any *outsider.*

When that's the case, you often are able to save the time and energy involved in explaining or supplying frequently difficult or convoluted background information.

Let us give you an example.

Suppose you wanted to write a memo to various department heads discussing a recent breach of security in the facility where we all work. In theory at least, each of the people who would be receiving the memo already has varying degrees of awareness and knowledge about the existing security system. Obviously, some will know more than others.

What are the givens in this situation?

Because this memo is being directed to department heads, you would start with the awareness that all will be somewhat familiar with the facility. All will be somewhat familiar with the security system. All will be somewhat familiar with the company's security policy. Granted, the degree of familiarity and background knowledge may vary from department head to department head. Nevertheless, you are starting on what can be considered far more common ground than would be the case with a group of outsiders totally unfamiliar with any aspect of the security system. What this means is that you don't have to cover quite as much background in order to begin a productive exchange of information.

On the other hand, if you were to discuss this breach of security with people unfamiliar with our company's security system, you would begin with the awareness that first you must explain the security system so that we can all work from the same data base, the same level of knowledge, and same background information. The key to making this document effective is to know the *audience* or *destination*. It doesn't have much to do with whether or not this is a *good news* or *bad news* situation.

Having presented our case for separation of documents, not by content but by audience and destination, let's proceed with our discussion of *internal* and *external* documents.

Internal Documents

Internal documents are documents which are not intended to be seen by anyone outside of the company or entity. They are internal use only. They come in all shapes, sizes, and lengths.

A short one-paragraph notice reminding everyone of the change in shift starting time during the holidays posted on bulletin boards all over the plant is an internal document.

A somewhat longer tri-fold piece of paper, perhaps color-coded with a different border and bearing a different style of print, is distributed with paychecks. This too is an internal document.

The annual budget, the annual business plan, the five-year marketing plan — in fact, the whole range and library of planning studies — are internal documents.

Yet if you ask most people what they think of when they are asked to identify internal documents (if they answer your question at all), they will most likely mention the workhorse of all internal documents, the memo.

So, let's talk about the memo first and then go on to other types of internal documents.

The Memo

The venerable old memo is the workhorse of internal correspondence. It can be as simple as a Post Office wanted poster.

Or, it can be as complicated (but probably not as lengthy) as the federal budget.

Memos are used to:

1. Make announcements.
2. Transmit more important documents.
3. Make assignments.
4. Delegate authority.
5. Grant approval.
6. Deny an application.
7. Call attention to some problem.
8. Convey favorable news.
9. Acknowledge...Follow up...prod...and more.

While the memo can handle a wide variety of assignments, it can also be presented in several different formats.

Formatting The Memo: 'Evident' or 'Subtle'

Two schools of thought exist on how best to organize the content of a memo. Also, there are any number of names for these approaches. There is the *evident* approach, which means that the memo gets straight to the point. Then there is the *subtle* approach, which means the author may choose to structure the document so the reader is regaled with information before the author gets to the point. Both formats have their merit, and both have their place in the scheme of things.

The 'Evident' Memo: Get To The Point

The example on the next page illustrates one important dimension of these documents that all memos have in common, the *subject* line. Regardless of whether the memo you are authoring is intended to be *up-front*, or if you want to take your time and sell your proposal first, you need a *subject* line.

Why? Because the whole purpose of the memo is to convey information, save time, and dispense with formalities that are only necessary when sending a document outside the hallowed walls of your company.

A *subject* line is both a short cut and a courtesy.

Your co-worker can pick up your memo, glance at the subject line, and decide whether to act on your memo now or put it away until later. In one case, your reader notes that your document is about the trailer park's admission policy and reads it immediately because the committee's decision affects some action the reader intends to take later in the day.

The 'Evident' Memo

December 11, 1999

TO: All Greystone Trailer Park Property
             Owners
FROM: Greystone Trailer Park Owner
             Association Committee
SUBJECT: Change In Park Lot Ownership Rules

In a 4 to 1 vote of the Greystone Park Rules Committee, the decision was made to lower the minimum age for ownership of property in Greystone park from 55 to 50 years of age. This change in Greystone Park by-laws becomes effective 1/1/2000.

Or, your reader has the option of laying the memo aside and digesting the contents later, when other matters are less pressing.

Suffice to say, when the intended audience for your memo picks up that piece of paper and reads the subject line, the reader should know immediately what your memo is about.

More About Memos

In the preceding example of a memo taken from the files of a trailer park in Florida, we have, in the same memo, an example of both what's good and what's bad about this venerable old form of corporate or company communication.

First, let's talk about the positive aspects of this memo. Obviously, this is an example of an *evident* memo.

The author doesn't waste any time getting to the point. These are memos where the subject of the memo and the first sentence (sometimes called the first sentence-paragraph) does a more than adequate job of telling the reader exactly what the memo is all about. Go back to look at the Greystone Trailer Park memo. Does the subject line in that memo tell its readers what the memo is about? The answer, of course, is yes.

Should the subject line be any different for a memo with a more subtle message? The answer, of course, is no. Why? Because the subject of the memo doesn't change, only the manner in which it is written.

The memo is strong in other ways as well. It is brief, informative, describes action taken, gives a timetable for implementation, and doesn't equivocate.

With so many things in its favor, why did we say it has its weak points as well?

The Greystone Trailer Park memo gives no background information. Why did the park lower its minimum ownership age? Why did it set the minimum age at 50 instead of 52 or 48? Why is the park waiting until the first of the year to implement the new by-laws?

These are legitimate questions. However, they are

beyond the scope and purpose of the original memo. The memo's purpose was only to convey specific information. Now the reader has that new knowledge. If the reader wants to know more, the reader must follow up.

In defense of the memo, consider what would have happened if the information about the change in by-laws had been buried in a lengthy document which focused on the discussion leading up to the changes. Readers might have given up on the lengthy piece of writing before they got to the most important part: the change in by-laws.

The 'Subtle' Memo: The Gentle Art Of Persuasion

Some people would find it all but impossible to write an *evident* memo, even though the situation called for one. If you are one of these, there is a memo form for you. The *subtle* memo is not quite as *in your face*.

The subtle memo is one that pleads its case to the reader. It presents you with a stream of logic. After considering this and that and weighing this and that, we have decided on A instead of B. In other words, subtle memos usually regale the reader with the logic behind the decision as well as the decision.

Are they as effective as the *evident* memo?

The answer is a definite perhaps.

If the only way you can author a memo is by being subtle, then by all means, be subtle. In the immortal words of Roger Sims, "It is better to have been subtly memoed than not memoed at all."

Students and seminar attendees frequently ask which we prefer. We have to respond honestly that we prefer the *evident* style. It gets the job done. It meets the criteria of effective business communication. An evident memo is concise, straightforward, to the point, and leaves no doubt in anyone's mind about the purpose of the memo. But you knew we would say this.

To critics of this often no frills, often blunt form of communication, who claim it leaves too many questions unanswered, we submit that brevity and clarity often inspire the asking of intelligent questions. Being mesmerized, manipulated, or entertained by someone's ability to disguise prose as logic and reason can actually stymie company communication.

Having said that, there are mechanical and formatting aspects of an effective memo.

Mechanical And Formatting Guides

BREVITY. Keep your memos brief. With few exceptions, you can write a memo of transmittal, make an announcement, pass out assignments, delegate authority, grant or deny approval, convey, or acknowledge very effectively with a single paragraph consisting of as few as two or as many as eight sentences.

FOCUS. One subject per memo. No more, no excuses. If you must discuss two issues, write two memos.

READABILITY. Studies repeatedly have shown that the most effective sentence length is anywhere from 8 to 11 words. Reader retention is highest with sentences of that length. By the same token, most folks need a micro-break after a six-to-eight sentence paragraph. A memo that is longer than four paragraphs begins to lose its effectiveness. A memo that is longer than four paragraphs or certainly more than one page is beginning to sound a whole lot like a report.

Write Tight and Right Tip

ANY TIME YOU AUTHOR A MEMO, KEEP
BREVITY, FOCUS, AND READABILITY
VERY MUCH IN MIND.

DISCUSSION. Not long ago while examining a business writing textbook written by the former CEO of a major airline, we noticed the author was building a case for the means of internal communication other than the memo. He declared the memo to be a poor substitute for a face-to-face discussion.

We agree. But remember that the memo was not designed or intended to replace good old-fashioned significant one-on-one dialogue. If it is being used in that fashion, it is being misused. The memo is the alternative of choice when that face-to-face is not possible.

The question remains: How are you going to communicate with a boss who is constantly on the road, located at another plant site, or, worse yet, halfway across the country? How are you going to convey certain information to your field sales force, off-site personnel, or someone who is too busy to sit down and talk to you? And, how can you be certain all of your people get the same message with the same words, the same emphasis, and at the same time?

A telephone will work in some cases. A video

conference will work in some cases. A regional meeting will work in some cases. But there are very few instances where a well-written memo won't hold the situation together until such time as a more desirable way to communicate is possible.

SOME CAUTIONS. One important thing to remember is that if a high degree of confidentiality is a premium, you will not achieve it if it is typed by someone other than yourself. If you don't want anyone else to see it besides the recipient, prepare the memo yourself. You seal it in some sort of envelope and mark it *confidential.* If the memo is handwritten, make it legible. In one company we know, an executive passed out handwritten memos like confetti. To top it off, he had illegible handwriting. Anyone getting one of his memos always had to check with him to verify what he meant.

It has been our experience that the *evident* (straight forward) kind of memo seems to work just fine in situations where you are passing along information that isn't likely to be upsetting. If you're going to inform someone that the person has just received an award, if you are acknowledging a stellar performance, if you liked the way a person authored a report or handled a meeting, then tell them right up front. But never start a memo "The purpose of this memo is to..." If you have to explain what your memo is about after authoring a subject line, you have not adequately defined your subject.

Finally, let's deal with the actual structure of an *evident* memo. Good memos have a format. Once you get on to that format, you'll have a way of checking the completeness and communication likelihood of your memo.

The 'Evident' Memo Format

If your memo is convoluted, complicated, or lengthy, consider formatting your memo as follows. In the first paragraph, state succinctly and explicitly your reason for sending the memo: "Congratulations to you and your people...," "Good job on the Foyster account...," "Thanks to you and your staff for...," or "Effective with the 8 a.m. shift..."

In the second paragraph, explain what needs to be explained. The most effective checklist we know of is to use the old journalistic one to see if you have covered all of the necessary dimensions of the situation: Who? What? Why? Where? When? How?

Finally, what involvements or ramifications are there for the reader? How will the information contained in this memo change someone's way of doing things, routines, the way things are looked at, a schedule, whatever. This is where you point that out.

The 'Subtle' Memo Format

While we are not proponents of the *subtle* memo, we do recognize that there are times when you really have no alternative. If you have to deliver *bad* news, we think you should do everything in your power to avoid sending it by memo. Don't fire someone by memo. Don't tell someone you can't approve a claim by memo. Don't tell someone by memo that he or she wasn't the one to receive the promotion. Bottom line: Don't send a memo in a bad news situation.

Walk down the hall to the person's office. Pick up the telephone.

First you cushion or buffer the bad news. Then you may decide to send a memo with all the gory details. But, by the time the memo gets there, some of the shock will have worn off. The sequencing followed in a *subtle* or *bad news* or *negative situation* memo is somewhat different than the format of an *evident* memo.

After you have confronted the recipient with the bad news, your first paragraph should have a cushioning effect. Instead of repeating the unpleasant message, review the conditions or circumstances leading up to the decision.

The second paragraph should reconfirm what the individual has already been told. You do this to avoid possible misunderstandings: "Yeah, I heard what you said but never dreamed that was what you meant."

Finally, you would write a third paragraph, if you believe that there is no possibility of reversal or reconsideration of the situation.

A Seldom Used Third Category Of Memo: The Request

In 99 of 100 cases, this type of memo is really no different than the *evident* memo discussed initially. It is similar in the sense that you are straightforward with the purpose of the memo. The difference is that you are requesting something as opposed to the more passive nature of telling someone this is *how it is*.

The second paragraph should fully explain what you need (want), and, if convenient to do so, explain why you need it: "The company is conducting a survey," or "We are establishing base line data," or whatever.

A third paragraph can be nothing more than a *courtesy* closing. Don't forget to say when you need the information. Don't forget to say *thank you*. Don't ask them to call you; you call them. Remember, you're the one who made the request.

Write Tight and Right Tip
IF YOU ARE SENDING A MEMO, IT'S A GOOD IDEA TO INITIAL THAT DOCUMENT NEXT TO YOUR NAME AT THE TOP OF THE MEMO. WHY? IT IS A WAY TO LET THE READER KNOW YOU HAVE DOUBLE-CHECKED ITS CONTENTS AND APPROVED THE MEMO.

The Memo: Summary

1. Memos can be used to make announcements, transmit documents, make assignments, delegate, approve, deny, call attention to problems, acknowledge, and much more.

2. There are two frequently used memo formats:
   - A.   *Evident* format, direct and straightforward, used in good news or informative situations.
   - B.   *Subtle* format, where the reasons for the action being taken are explained prior to announcing change.

3. Memo formats consist of:
  A. Date:
  B. To:
  C. From:
  D. Subject:
  E. Text.

4. A well-structured memo will:
  A. Address only one topic per memo.
  B. Use a sentence length of 8 to 11 words.
  C. Contain paragraphs of six to eight sentences.
  D. Have a length of no more than one page.

5. A well-constructed memo is brief, focused, and readable.

6. Guard against the memo becoming the primary means of communication within the entity. Rather, it should be viewed as merely one more of the communication tools available to you and a way to augment other forms of communication.

7. A third and less frequently used memo form is the *request* format. *Request* memos require some form of follow-up response from the recipient.

Practical Practice #13

KEEPING THE GUIDELINES TO EFFECTIVE, TIGHTLY
WRITTEN, INTERNAL DOCUMENTS IN MIND,
CONSIDER THE FOLLOWING PROBLEM.

During a recent EEO investigation, you discover that
the company that recently employed you as Employment
Manager has not followed long-established government
guidelines relating to public display of a non-sexual harassment
policy. (By law, this policy, complete with your company's
definitions of sexual harassment, must be printed on all
employment forms.)

You inform the Human Resources Manager of this
oversight, and she in turn tells you that she wants you to draft
the wording for such a policy. But first she wants you to define
"sexual harassment."

"Define the term," she tells you, "and then draft a sexual
harassment policy statement that can be printed on all
employment materials. The statement should be brief,
comprehensive, and written so that all applicants and employees
can understand it."

After defining the term, how would you word such a
statement?

Practical Practice #14

KEEPING THE GUIDELINES TO EFFECTIVE, TIGHTLY
WRITTEN, INTERNAL DOCUMENTS IN MIND,
CONSIDER THE FOLLOWING PROBLEM.

You are the president of a young and growing company. Growth has exceeded forecast for the past five years. Profits are good and the future looks promising.

Then something happens. You notice that key department heads are starting to bicker, absenteeism is increasing, product sales have begun to decline, customer complaints are increasing, and, for the first time in company history, profits have declined for two straight quarters. If this trend continues, the company will lose a substantial amount of money.

In your talks with various department heads, each blames someone else for their problems. Quality blames engineering. Engineering blames sales. Sales blames pricing. No one seems to be doing his or her job. Finally you are informed that your major customer is considering canceling its contract and shifting its business to your major competitor. The loss of this contract would necessitate laying off more than half of your skilled workforce.

In desperation you hire a consultant who, after six weeks of investigation, informs you he has never encountered such an "I don't care" attitude. He recommends that you develop a course of remedial actions. Then you must author a corporate manifesto in which you outline actions you want to take place as well as a timetable for implementing these corrections. Ultimately you will share the contents of this document with each department head.

In the real world, your task is to first prepare a list of corrective actions, and establish goals and timetables for completion of these actions. **The most important part of your task will be to communicate these goals and timetables to your staff.** You decide that this can best be accomplished with an internal document that explains the gravity of the situation, and calls for a series of one-on-one meetings with each department head to discuss these corrective actions and their completion dates.

Keeping in mind what the authors have said about the construction of internal documents, prepare a **draft** of your communication focusing on clarity, brevity, and at the same time, conveying a very real sense of urgency. (**Goal: 250 words**)

A Different Kind of 'Internal' Document: The Report

At the opposite end of the spectrum from the humble memo in the land of internal documents is something called the *report*. What's the difference?

Think of them this way. On the surface at least, a memo is relatively short. The report is, for the most part, usually longer and likely to be on the more formal side.

In reality, the differences are more meaningful, but length and formality are as good a place as any to make the initial distinction.

Okay, it's longer and more formal. Let's talk about some other ways to categorize reports. One way certainly is to point to the report's purpose. Some reports are designed to give your coworkers information (remember these are internal documents). Another type of report, written in a slightly different style, may have a different purpose: The analysis of a situation so the problem or condition is better understood. Still another report may, through its presentation, be designed to persuade you and your fellow employees to take some action or embrace some business goal or philosophy that replaces the old with the new.

In other words, reports have almost as many different uses as memos. But there is one big difference: Reports take a lot longer to write.

Some reports may be written in *an evident* fashion just like their cousins in the memo format. In other words, the straightforward approach explains what happened or an outcome: Here is why it happened the way it did.

Just as a memo can be written in a *subtle* format where the document explains the reasons why a certain conclusion is reached before announcing the conclusion, reports can be written in the same fashion.

By now you may be thinking, so far the only real difference between memos and reports I've heard you mention is length. If that's the case, let me point out that in the majority of cases, reports are written by more than one author. It is not uncommon to have reports written by a team assembled for the specific purpose of writing the report.

Let us give you an example. Every year, on the first day of September at one company, an employee from each of the firm's areas — marketing, finance, manufacturing, engineering, quality assurance, purchasing, sales, and personnel — was assembled to write a business plan for the upcoming fiscal year. In the preliminary stages of assembling this plan, the mission, goals, and objectives of each department were addressed and discussed by representatives of that particular area. Not until the final draft did one person take over the writing chore. And the only reason that was done was to give the document what is known as a common voice.

However, there is still another difference between a memo and a report besides the length and possible number of authors: That is what is known as the peripheral components of the report.

Many reports are supported by visual aids, graphs, hand-made prototypes, and maybe some other formality in presentation (all the way up to being presented in the form of a booklet) that can and often requires an oral presentation.

For at least the last 20 years when this annual business plan was being authored by representatives of the division's various departments, there was a week of careful preparation — all designed to unveil the plan for the senior officers of the corporation.

One wag explained the differences between a memo and a report this way: "If it can't be confined to one page, it's probably a report."

The First Distinction

An *informative* report usually focuses on events such as a new product launching, the election of a new board of directors, the opening of a branch office, the findings of a prolonged investigation, or any other situation where employees are presented with organized data, facts, or knowledge.

If you author a report that is essentially an informative report, your objective should be to present that information in an unbiased, understandable, objective, complete, reliable, and truthful fashion. It is not your job to manipulate that data in any way, shape, or form. Certainly you have no responsibility to sway opinions or decisions. If your report meets all the criteria described, your co-workers, after reading the information-driven report, should be able to arrive at an equally objective understanding of the situation.

The *analytical* report is different. Here the author(s) of the report have a different agenda. In an analytical report, the author's mission is to give the readers (co-workers, audience) objectively evaluated information without forcing a conclusion on his readers. Again, an example.

Several years ago, a company opened a West Coast facility, a duplication of a successful East Coast operation. For a period of twelve months, a supervisory group studied potential customers' material purchase patterns, assessed freight rates, plotted demand curves, analyzed foreign metal pricing, developed potential supply sources, studied the labor market, and examined information from every possible angle. Then, when the group had massaged all of this material into a readable, 47-page document, complete with exhibits and a video presentation, they presented their analysis to corporate officers who approved or disapproved capital expenditures required to launch an effort of that magnitude. That corporate decision, the group realized, would be based on their analysis. If their analysis were faulty, the corporation stood to lose a lot of money. If it were on target, the estimates of return on investment would far exceed corporate guidelines.

Let's boil this discussion of informative and analytical reports down to this. An informative report is usually generated to explain why something has happened. An analytical report, more often than not, is generated to make something happen.

Write Tight and Right Tip

IF YOU HAVE A REPORT TO WRITE, GET BUSY NOW. DON'T WAIT UNTIL THE LAST MINUTE TO START BECAUSE A WELL-WRITTEN REPORT REQUIRES FORETHOUGHT, RESEARCH, AND PLAN-NING. ONLY THEN ARE YOU PREPARED TO BEGIN WRITING.

Everything Starts With Thinking

All right, now you know the purpose of your report. You know what you want your audience to do and what you expect to achieve with this document that you are about to author. Now you make some mental notes for yourself.

Let us give you an example.

Your immediate supervisor, the food editor for a large metropolitan newspaper, has instructed you to conduct a study of area restaurants with an eventual eye (perhaps) toward publishing an area dining guide. "Put a preliminary report together for the editorial staff's assessment," she tells you.

Where do you start?

The first question you have to ask yourself is what type of report? Is it informative? Is it analytical? Or, is it a combination of both? The answer, like so many tasks we are asked to define, is that at this point it isn't really clear. Since your boss used the term *staff assessment*, you are probably going to lean toward the informative approach. Still, it does have the ring of analytical about it as well, doesn't it? What to do? Whatever you do, the important thing is to get started, realizing that sooner rather than later you need to be thinking about what kind of report you will eventually construct.

Starting off, you need answers to some basic questions. Who will be reading this report? Answer: Other members of the editorial staff.

Second question: How will your report be used? Early indications are that the editorial staff will look at what you have to decide if they want to proceed with the dining guide project.

Third question: (Don't be afraid to ask a question.)

Ask: What type of information does your editor want to see in this preliminary report?

Caution: Don't just blunder into your boss' office and blurt out something like, "Just exactly what do you want to see in this report?" Instead, think the matter through and reason out what kind of information you would need if you were going to make the decision. Then when your editor responds with something like, "Well, Mel (or Melody), what kind of information do you think we should be gathering?" you'll have some ideas and some answers. Believe us, your editor will be much more impressed with that than she would be if you shrug your shoulders or say something like, "Boy, that's a tough one, boss. What do you think?"

Think about this: If you can recite a list of items you believe would make the restaurant guide more appealing and informative, your editor will be more likely to think she made the right choice when she selected you for the assignment.

In other words, even though on the surface it may appear that you have been given an information gathering assignment, make and keep careful notes on the peripheral data of your study. Those observations and interpretations could prove to be valuable if you suddenly find your assignment has evolved into an analytical report.

Whenever we have been called upon to do a report of any substance, we made it a point to try to schedule a brainstorming session with our boss. In the verbal give and take that followed, we usually discovered that he had a rather clear concept of what he wanted, or what he felt needed to be done. That made it easier. Having a good idea of what the boss wanted done usually pointed us in the right direction.

Let us offer three tips to the novice report writer.

FIRST TIP: If you know that someone has recently authored a report for your boss and you are able to determine that the report was well received, ask to see a copy of it. Needless to say, you are not interested in content; you are interested in format. If the format in that report will work for you, then there is no need to re-invent the wheel.

SECOND TIP: No matter what the due date — tomorrow, six weeks from tomorrow — get started immediately, even if you have to initiate your study while wrapping up some previous assignment. Putting off getting started on a newly assigned report is one of the seven deadly corporate writing sins.

THIRD TIP: If you haven't been sworn to secrecy, discuss your project with your corporate peers. They may have ideas or be able to offer some perspective that will help you start.

Organize Your Data Gathering

By now you've probably figured how you're going to proceed. So now you have a fairly good idea what information you need for this report, where you can get the data, and how you plan to go about gathering it. So, if your question is as simple as where are the best places to eat in your area, where do you start?

Classic information-gathering techniques start with first tapping the most immediate and available sources of information. In this case, that would be the people in your own company.

Makes sense, doesn't it? No sophisticated data gathering techniques, no lengthy questionnaires. Just you and a note pad, tapping the sources inside your own company. Talk to 20 people. Tell them you want the names of their favorite restaurant, and you're off and running. While you're at it, check the newspaper library. More than likely, someone at sometime has already looked into something along this line in the past. Remember the old saying: No new idea is 100 percent new.

Then, when you think you've depleted your inside sources, turn to the outside world.

Turn to the Yellow Pages of the phone book. Look at the display ads. Call the convention bureau; see what restaurants they recommend. Find out where people do their business entertaining. Check with the Chamber of Commerce. Find out where the ethnic food restaurants are located. Are they in Greektown, or Chinatown, or in the Italian section, or wherever. These are often hidden culinary treasures.

Or, why not call a couple of the local food distributors? Tell them you want to know who buys the best cuts of meat, the freshest seafood, the highest quality supplies. You'll probably be surprised at how much information is available to you.

Depending on the subject and nature of your report, the quantity and quality of research data available on most any subject in the '90s is mind-bending. Today even small town libraries can provide you with special encyclopedias, videotapes, workbooks, handbooks, manuals, technical publications, journals, government reports, and computer generated data. The list goes on. Whatever your subject matter, wherever you are, the age of electronics has brought the world of information to your doorstep, not to mention the rich resources of Internet and Netscape.

Finally, you begin to see the patterns. Ideas and

strategies for presenting the data are starting to develop. Without realizing it you are beginning to sort through what at first appeared to be just a morass of facts, figures, and details. Here you gain a piece of logic, there a fragment of solid information. When you think you have searched long enough, get started. If you haven't done enough research, it will soon be apparent.

Formatting The Formal Business Report

Okay, now you understand your assignment because you've had a couple of conversations with your boss about what is expected when your report is received. Not only that, you know why the report is asked for and you know how the information will be used.

At this point, you have either done or know how you're going to wrap up your research. In other words, you're ready to write. Right?

Let's talk about the format of a formal business report. For the moment, let's underline that word *formal*.

The reality of corporate communications is that all reports are not formal. Every day, in hundreds of ways, people discuss reports with people. Those reports may be nothing more than a handful of handwritten notes. Across the hall, someone else may be reading several days' accumulation of facts gathered from a phone campaign, all contained in a three-ring notebook. Down the hall, someone is reciting facts scribbled on scraps of paper.

What's our point?

Our point is that these examples are not formal reports. This point does not make the information contained in these *informal* reports any less important than their documented counterparts; it is simply that up until this point, no one has requested that the report be massaged into something more formal.

To formalize your report then, you are going to have to at least consider producing or constructing the following report components:

1. a memo of transmittal.
2. a cover page for your report.
3. an executive summary.
4. the text of the report.
5. appropriate exhibits.
6. glossary (if necessary).
7. bibliography (if necessary).

First, let's defuse the specter of what might look to some people like an overwhelming and decidedly bureaucratic task. Even the most formal of formal business reports seldom contains all the components listed above.

Nevertheless, we'll review all of these components, some in more depth than others, on the remote chance that you might have to deal with one someday.

The Memo of Transmittal

We covered the subject of memos in the early part of this section. It won't take a rocket scientist to determine that the memo that goes with a formal report is very much an evident memo.

The message of the memo of transmittal is short and sweet: "Here is the report you requested. It's done."

Exhibit 1: Memo of Transmittal

November 11, 1999

TO: Roberta Eggers
FROM: Ted Lawson
SUBJECT: 1999 Area Restaurant Survey

Ms. Eggers, the survey you requested is now complete and a copy of the report is attached.

If after reviewing the report, you or any other members of the editorial staff would like to review some of the support material, call me and I will bring the files to your office.

Questions?

Short and simple. Brief and to the point. So brief, in fact, that some may even question why it is necessary.

The answer is that it is *proof* you not only finished the report on time and as requested, but you sent it through proper channels to the person who requested the report.

In our experience in marketing and sales, our staff was instructed to include a memo of transmittal with every formal document. Less formal reports were treated somewhat more casually; a hand-written note stapled to the corner of the document often would suffice. You need to be alert to the business culture where you are, of course.

To us, that memo of transmittal always has been a "feel good" piece of paper. To us, it meant that the project was done and on its way; it was off the list of things to do.

As we noted, whether or not you and your company choose to see that your reports are accompanied by a memo of transmittal is a matter of corporate culture. But, if the boss wants them, you better know how to write one and when to use one.

The Cover Page

Cover pages are not brain surgery and yet we have seen and continue to see botched up cover pages on reports.

The cover sheet of the report is a sheet of paper containing the name of the report, the author of the report, and the date of the report. Depending on the sensitivity of the document, you may have the word *confidential* written on it.

Exhibit 2: Cover Page

**1999
AREA RESTAURANT SURVEY**

**BY
TED LAWSON
ROGER SIMS**

NOVEMBER 11, 1999

The Executive Summary

Back in high school or college when you first learned to construct a formal report, this part was the page most people called the *abstract*.

In business, this page is called the *executive summary*. The page usually is written in one of two ways.

One way is to be brief. By brief, we mean no more than a 100-word summary. These short and sweet capsule summaries are written tightly. They are a way for senior executives in the firm to glance at the report, see what it is about, and then determine whether they want to go through the report itself. A 100-word executive summary takes about 1/3 of the page and it is the only thing that appears on that page.

We are aware of one large firm that makes available the executive summary of all reports published the previous day. All the manager has to do is turn on his electric work station and be updated. If any manager wants to see some report, the report then can be called up on the monitor.

A second but far less frequently used type of executive summary is the expanded summary or synopsis. These summaries typically are three to four pages in length and may even include an outline of the report.

In either case, the executive summary usually is found on the first page, immediately following the cover page.

Exhibit 3: Executive Summary

Executive Summary

1999
Area Restaurant Survey

This report, written by Ted Lawson and Roger Sims of Bayview Publishing Research Department for Senior Editor Roberta Eggers, is a survey of Cass, Fortense, Plagger, and Duo County Restaurants as well as the Mongrain metropolitan area.

This report covers 129 restaurants, divided into 10 categories, including price, service, hours, cleanliness, variety, parking, accessibility, bar, handicap accommodations, and atmosphere.

The report is 22 pages long and is available on Code 23 VRT.

The Text Or Body Of The Report

As with any report, paper, analysis, examination of an issue, or, as in this case, a restaurant survey, your document has three essential parts:

1. The introduction.
2. The body.
3. The ending.

Introduction

Every report starts somewhere, usually with an *idea* or a *need*. This genesis is important, because it tells your reader why this report was constructed. Someone, somewhere, had a need, wanted to know something, or, of course, the reasons are endless. The introduction makes clear who authorized the report, who actually constructed the report, and defines the limits of the report.

One or two paragraphs of good tight writing should give your readers all the background information they need to understand the purpose and scope of the report. If your introduction is more than one page, do some serious editing and revising. Background is history, and history, especially in the world of business, is prologue.

Get on with the report.

The Body Of The Document

This is it. This is *the report*. This is where you present your data, your information, your objective analysis — and in some cases you will be asked for your subjective views as well — and your discussion.

Depending on the style that your supervisors or department heads prefer, the report is either written with the pronoun-free style of a resume, or the more personal, almost conversational style of the interoffice communication. In either case, you need to know which writing style is preferred. If style preference isn't obvious, review some previous reports to see how they were written.

In most cases, the author(s) of a report are expected to give their assessment of the data. It doesn't make much sense to assign a valued employee to a project — read this as one who is trusted enough to conduct the study in the first place — and then not listen to the report writer's opinion.

Still, the question arises, what should I include in the report? How do I know when I've taken the report far enough?

There is no clear-cut, definitive answer to either question.

The best answer we've come up with is that if you had requested this report, what information would you want it to contain? In other words, if you were going to read this report and you wanted information about a particular restaurant, what information would that be? Then ask yourself whether that information is contained in the report. If it isn't, include it.

If you have included the information you were instructed to obtain — and you have included information that fleshes out the report — chances are your report accomplishes its goals. Before you start expecting applause for a job well done, however, remember this: No report, no matter how carefully constructed, covers everything. Someone, somewhere, is going to want answers to a question your report probably could have but did not address. It is the job of a report to raise not only the reader's level of knowledge or awareness but to raise more questions as well. What's that old saying: "Inquiring minds want to know?"

The Conclusion

There are at least two ways to wrap up a formal report, and the one you use depends on what kind of report you are generating:

1. Summary or conclusion.
2. Author's recommendations.

Summary, Conclusion...Which?

The thing you must remember about a summary is that the author of a report never includes any new information in the summary. If your report is quite lengthy (more than 25 pages), it is a good idea to have a brief summary at the end of each section of the report. These mini-summaries are especially helpful if the report leans toward the technical side.

A conclusion is a little different. Here, a word of caution as well. The conclusion has to be based on the facts presented in the text of the report. Author bias should have no impact whatsoever on the conclusion.

Maybe A Recommendation?

There are reports where some document-ending action other than a summary or conclusion is appropriate. Instead of a rehashing of the report's finer points, some answers to some questions will be obvious to the author. Where is the best place to eat if you want seafood? Where is the best place to dine if you want French country cooking? What's the best deal for a family of four? Who makes good vichyssoise in the area? These questions call for recommendations.

Recommendations need to include sufficient qualifying on the part of the author so that the reader has a realistic idea of what to expect when entering the restaurant.

Write Tight and Right Tip

IN LONGER, TECHNICAL REPORTS, IT IS COMMON TO FIND A TABLE OF CONTENTS. IF YOU BELIEVE A TABLE OF CONTENTS WILL MAKE IT EASIER FOR THE READER TO DIGEST YOUR REPORT OR GET THE INFORMATION DESIRED, INCLUDE ONE. INSERT IT BETWEEN THE COVER PAGE AND THE EXECUTIVE SUMMARY.

Exhibits

In the past, while many reports will have an occasional graph or chart interspersed throughout the report, the large majority of reports save this type of *visual* material for a section of the report near the end. The advent of desktop publishing has made these materials far more accessible than in the past. Today, the ease with which they can be readily folded into the text has made it possible to place them almost anywhere in the report the author deems appropriate.

So, while charts and graphs may still be occasionally found in the *exhibits* portion of the report, be aware that they also can be woven into the theme of the text.

When this is the case, the exhibits portion of your report may be reduced to duplicating and presenting survey questionnaires, reproducing (in this case) menus, maps, contact information, photographs, etc.

In discussing the construction of the exhibits section of a formal report, one of the most frequent questions we hear is, "What goes in the exhibits section?" To us, two answers make sense.

1. If you believe it belongs in the text of the report because it sheds light on some aspect of that report, but you don't know where to put it, the exhibits section probably is okay.
2. Anything that doesn't go somewhere else.

Remember, we told you it would make sense.

Glossary

According to <u>Webster's</u> <u>Dictionary</u>, a glossary is a list of difficult, old, technical, or foreign words with explanations "...usually found at the end of the text."

While the words in our restaurant survey may not meet this rather terse definition, that doesn't mean the reader doesn't need to know what we mean when a restaurant uses a term, particularly on their menu, that is unfamiliar.

Over the years, we have written reports on a variety of subjects. We have discovered that the more uncommon the subject matter, the more likely the list of glossary entries will be lengthy.

Our suggestion is, after you have completed the text of the report, have a colleague read your report and underline those terms with which he or she is not completely familiar. Then, after you have reviewed the words, it's up to you to decide if those terms need to be defined.

We cannot always assume that our superiors, peers, or subordinates — in this case, the editorial staff — know any more about the intricacies of the restaurant world than you do. In fact, they may not know as much; after all, you're the one who just completed the survey.

Finally, if your report is of a technical nature, particularly one that involves new technology, it is almost certain that some sort of glossary will be needed. In any case, if you need them, they are not difficult to construct. Just follow the model in your dictionary.

Finally, The Bibliography

Remember those painful *bibliography* and *works cited* pages at the conclusion of research papers back in college? Well, now you know that they weren't putting you through all that grief for nothing. There really are occasions when you need to know how to construct a bibliography.

The need for a bibliography seems to raise its head most frequently when a report is devoted to policy review or formation, either corporate or government. A marketing report which relies on demographic studies or a technical report or analysis which uses prior research material will also require the authors to cite their sources.

If you cite statistics, refer to previous studies or reports, or quote from previously published sources, you should include a bibliography at the end of your report.

Trying to cover all of the possible works cited situations that might arise would fill several pages. This workbook is certainly no place to try to enlighten a novice report writer on the ins and outs, rules and regulations, and do's and don'ts of a bibliography. Suffice to say, if one is required, talk to your librarian. Have your librarian suggest any one of a number of readily available writers' handbooks that illustrate the appropriate format for recording the bibliography at the end of a formal business report. Or, again, look at previously accepted reports for guidelines.

The Report: Summary

1. Compared to a memo, a report is substantially longer, decidedly more formal, and is usually authored by more than one person. Unlike the memo, the report is often accompanied by visual aids, graphs, and sometimes an oral presentation.

2. For the most part, reports can be categorized as *informative* or *analytical*. Informative reports are designed to help explain something. Analytical reports are designed to make something happen.

3. Before you put pen to paper, ask yourself who will be reading this report? Then, ask yourself how the report will be used? Finally, find out what the readers of your report are expecting to see.

4. Three tips for the novice report writer:
   a. Review known successful reports in your company.
   b. Get started immediately.
   c. If not sworn to secrecy, discuss the project with co-workers to generate ideas.

5. Most formal business reports contain the following:
   a. Memo of transmittal.

      b.   Cover page.
      c.   Executive summary.
      d.   The body of the report.
      e.   Exhibits (optional).
      f.   Glossary (optional).
      g.   Bibliography (optional).

6.   The body of the report should have:
      a.   Introduction.
      b.   The subject matter of the report.
      c.   Summary, conclusion, or recommendations.

7.   Exhibits may include examples of research methods, tests, questionnaires, visual aids, graphs, charts, maps, or photos.

8.   A glossary is not required for all business reports. A glossary becomes necessary, however, when some terms used in the report are likely to be unfamiliar to the reader.

9.   Bibliographies are required in a formal business report when the author(s) cite statistics or quote from previously published sources.

Visual Aids

Whether you are wrapping up your report, dropping it in an envelope and mailing it along with a memo of transmittal, or getting ready to make an oral presentation, consider the subject of *visual aids*. A visual aid can be:

Clip art. Slide(s). Photograph(s). Model(s). Map(s). Chart(s). Drawing(s). Graph(s). Prototype(s).

Or, the presentation of your report can even be augmented by videos or movies.

In other words, just about anything that is going to help your audience understand and remember what it is you have to say can be considered a visual aid.

Any list of cautions in helping the individual decide whether or not to use visual aids to augment a report is going to include the following:

1. Know the type of equipment your visuals will require. Do a full rehearsal to make certain everything works. Is the electrical cord long enough to operate from anywhere in the room? Do you have a spare bulb?

2. When you present visual information in slides or graphs, give your audience time to digest it. If the information requires explanation, explain it. Don't assume your audience understands.

3.   It doesn't work to circulate visuals, models, prototypes, supporting documents, or other materials while you are presenting the text of your report either orally or visually. One of two things will happen: Your audience will become absorbed in the visual and miss your presentation, or your presentation will have moved on to another point and the significance of your prop will be lost.

4.   Flip charts always work better if they are prepared prior to the presentation. Consider color to enhance the impact of your charts.

5.   Make certain your visuals are consistent with your presentation. If you are giving a formal presentation, your aids to understanding should lean toward the formal side. Don't mix humorous and serious visuals. When you do, your audience gets confused about how to respond.

6.   The only kind of visual aid that works is one that is uncluttered, readily understandable, and relevant. Consider the following item from the

February 9, 1990 edition of <u>The</u> <u>Wall</u> <u>Street</u> <u>Journal</u>:

> "SEVENTY-FIVE PERCENT OF NEW JOBS CREATED BETWEEN 1990 AND 2000 WILL DEMAND REPORT WRITING AND PUBLIC SPEAKING ABILITIES."

Some Comments About Electronic Mail

A young man once approached one of the authors after a writing seminar and asked what we thought about E-mail. More specifically, he said, "What does the acceptance of E-mail do to all your theories about writing?"

The author looked at him and smiled. "If ever anything was going to come along that would point out the need for people to master written business communications, it was E-mail," was the answer.

The young man, slightly perplexed by the answer, asked, "How?"

"Suddenly, everyone who authors anything and sends it out over the E-mail system will have 1,001 critical editors. When it comes to E-mail, not just the single recipient of your memo is going to see that you haven't mastered business communication, but every Tom, Dick, Harry, and Helen is going to see it as well," was the not-too-flippant answer.

The young man gulped.

"Paranoia will destroy ya," he was reminded. The truth of the matter is, if ever there were a device or system that will highlight the weakness in an individual's writing skills, E-mail will. That grammar whiz typist who used to check and correct all of your correspondence efforts before you sent them out is no longer in the loop.

The second thing to keep in mind is that despite E-mail's tremendous acceptance since the early '80s and the corresponding reduction in component and system cost, we are some distance from living in a world where E-mail systems are the rule rather than the exception.

The combination of conventional mail, TWX, Telex, and facsimile services still accounts for the major share of our business correspondence in interorganizational mail. E-mail's impact on intraorganizational communication is far more significant, accounting, one recent study showed, for fully 25 percent of all internal correspondence and the figure is climbing fast.

The business slow-down of the late '80s and early '90s forced a number of firms to put their plans for an E-mail system installation on the back burner. The capital outlay for not only the unit cost of printers, display units, imaging systems, and keyboards — not to mention cost of installation and user training — was coupled with the oft-unanswered questions about unattended reception, simultaneous message preparation and transmission, the need for system compatibility, and system security. Add to that questions about system safety and system reliability and E-mail, even with a total communication system capability, still hasn't replaced the author of that all-important internal document.

Write Tight and Right Tip
MOST BUSINESS AUDIENCES ARE LOOKING
FOR PRACTICAL INFORMATION, FRESH
APPROACHES, AND SOUND IDEAS. FORGET
THAT WHICH IS IRRELEVANT.

PART IV

EXTERNAL DOCUMENTS

Let's Talk About External Documents

First, we are going to talk about something you know. Then, we are going to discuss a couple of things you may not have thought about.

The thing that you know is that when we're talking about external documents, we are talking about those official papers, instruments, records, chronicles, and business letters that leave your place of business and are read by people who are not part of your inner-workings, organization, structure, consortium, combine — whatever you call yourself.

Okay, now we are working from a common definition.

Let's turn our attention to some things you may not have thought about.

If you are sending out a piece of correspondence with your company's letterhead on it and if the recipient has never heard of your company before, what does that recipient know about your company?

The answer: The only thing that recipients know about your company is what they read (or see) in that letter. If a person sees a letter that is poorly organized, what does that person think of your company?

If someone reads your letter and that letter has been sent out with one or two misspelled words and a couple of grammatical errors in it, what impression does the recipient get of your company?

Suppose a customer gets a letter from someone in your company and the customer's name has been misspelled. What is the customer supposed to think if the letter has strike-overs, whiteouts, or words omitted?

The answer in each case is that most people are uneasy about companies that tolerate and permit such things. They are not certain about whether or not they want to do business with a firm that can't even author a simple business letter.

Have we made our point?

If we haven't, let us give you something else to think about.

First of all, we are not grammarians; the quality of our lives does not hinge on correct comma placements, avoiding split infinitives, or fearing dangling participles. As individuals charged with writing business letters, our concern and your happiness (job satisfaction) shouldn't depend on such matters either.

Your concern should focus on the question: Did you author a letter that accomplishes what you want it to accomplish? Did your reader (customer?) understand what you said? Did you make yourself clear?

To prove our point, we sometimes conduct this little test. We take each piece of business correspondence received during a one-week period and evaluate it. The last time we did this test, at the end of that week, we had received 11 business letters, 3 organizational announcements, 6 brochures, 9 advertising pieces, a couple of notes from friends, and a stack of junk mail.

The notes and junk mail we'll forget. The other pieces we'll examine.

Every one of the business letters and the organizational announcements contained at least one error. One of the announcements contained no less than seven errors.

So, what's the big deal?

If you are one of those individuals who has worked night and day for years to build your company, paid untold dollars to some advertising or public relations company to create a logo and image, hammered on the theme of quality, struggled to insure and assure on-time delivery, it's safe to say you don't want some less-than-professional individual undoing all your hard work by sending out correspondence (with your company's name on it) that isn't consistent with the image you have worked so hard to achieve.

On the other hand, if you are presently one of those individuals working for one of the companies described above but entertaining hopes of becoming a captain of your own industry, there is no better time than now to learn to correspond with people. It is a skill that few people have taken the time to hone and master.

Getting Focused

For the next several pages, we want to focus on the anatomy of a simple business letter.

Whether or not this is good news or bad news or a sales letter, all distinctions that many text books on business writing like to make, is not important — at least not at this time.

The qualities of a good business letter are the same as those of a good memo. Just as a successful memo depends in large measure on the thoroughness of the preparation cycle (planning, organizing, and focusing) your business letter depends on the same elements. But — and we hasten to add the all-important but — there are also some major differences.

Like the memo, your audience is the most important consideration in your letter. Before you put pen to paper, you

ask yourself the same questions you had to ask when you wrote
the memo. Questions such as "How much background do I
need to supply?" need answers. How will the recipients of this
letter view what is being said? Will they like it? Will they
agree? Will they disagree? Will they have to respond? Will
they have to take action as the result of your letter?

Even when you know the answers to the questions
outlined above, you still have other factors to consider. For
example, is a business letter the best way to approach or
document this particular situation? Would you be better off to
call the person and then write the letter to:

1. Confirm the contents of your conversation,

And at the same time,

2. Reaffirm the agreed upon course of action?

On the other hand, do you even need a letter? Perhaps a
phone call would handle the situation. The answer, of course,
depends on whether a phone call can handle the matter, or
whether it requires documentation.

However, for the purpose of keeping our discussion
focused and avoiding straying into other not so relevant
considerations, let's say that you have decided that you are
going to write a letter, and that you know what you intend to
say. If there is any doubt in your mind as to what those
considerations should be, go back and read again the section on
memos in the internal documents section of this workbook.

The Parts Of A Typical Business Letter

In order, they are:

1. The date.
2. Address of recipient.
3. The salutation.
4. The text of the letter.
5. The closing.
6. The signature.
7. Enclosure statement (if needed).

Now, let's look at these components piece by piece, part by part, starting with the date.

The Date

The date should always be the date the letter is prepared. If time is critical, let the postmark on the envelope handle that. Avoid the temptation to falsify the date of the letter for whatever purpose it might serve you. We know of one case where lawyers proved that a client of an insurance company falsified the dates on a letter that accompanied the questionnaire in an insurance investigation.

"If he lied about the date," the insurance investigator claimed, "he'll lie about other things."

The court referee bought the argument. The questionnaire was deemed suspect, and the client's claim was denied.

Inside Address Or Contact Information

This one is simple. Obviously, if you are writing your letter on company stationery, the matter of the inside address has already been addressed. (Sorry, we couldn't resist.) On the other hand, if your business letter is being prepared on plain white bond, then you should make certain your letter has the appropriate inside address or contact information that will permit the reader to respond to the author of the letter. That's assuming you want to guarantee that the recipient of your letter knows where to respond.

If not, don't.

There are occasions when you do not want to include your return address in a letter. Understand that it is perfectly permissible to send a business letter without return contact information, but the situations are infrequent and the practice of not including it should be the exception rather than the rule.

If you do include a return address, you have two options about where to place this information. You can place it on the left hand side of your letter, immediately under the date, or you can place it on the right hand side opposite the address of the person to whom the letter is addressed. Either placement is perfectly acceptable.

Exhibit 1:   Placing Inside Address On Left Side

November 15, 1999

Casper A. Tinsley
8881 Tarmack Road
Chensworth, IN 46719

Rev. Cain Blackman
First Church of Big Miracles
8675 Salten Road
Land of Lakes, MN 77132

Exhibit 2:   Placing Inside Address On Right Side

November 15, 1999

> Casper A. Tinsley
> 8881 Tarmack Road
> Chensworth, IN 46719

Rev. Cain Blackman
First Church of Big Miracles
8675 Salten Road
Land of Lakes, MN 77132

The placement of the inside address is up to you, unless your company dictates one style or the other. For our own preference, in cases where the stationery does not have a preprinted legend or logo, we like the inside address on the right side of the page. To us, it looks just a bit less cluttered.

About The Address Of The Recipient

In this case:

> *Rev. Cain Blackman*
> *First Church of Big Miracles*
> *8675 Salten Road*
> *Land of Lakes, MN 77132*

As business addresses go, this is one of the simpler ones. Consider the following:

> *Ms. Nancy Portiskowski*
> *Director of Continuing Education*
> *Student Services*
> *Creighton-Loftman Center for Arts & Sciences*
> *Creighton College*
> *Handover Blvd. Building A, Suite 3118*
> *6220 Stadium Drive*
> *Clinton, KS 61616-5171*

The faster we go, the more complicated our mailing addresses become. Also, of course, the more likely we are to make a mistake in trying to make contact.

Is the spelling of the name correct?

Is the person's title correct (and current)?

Which building? Which suite? What about the zip code?

If you think we're overstressing the point, consider this: The Postal Service estimates that nearly 2 million pounds of mail are undeliverable on any given day. The biggest reason? Improper address.

Get in the habit of not just checking, but double checking. When you do, you'll discover that two things have started to happen. One, there are fewer *little* mistakes happening around the office; and, two, when people know you are watching the details, they'll begin to watch them too.

If you want to irritate clients (or customers), misspell their names.

If you want to further irritate them, neglect their title or use the wrong one when you refer to them. People work hard for their positions. They are proud of their titles and the least you can do is get it right.

But you knew all of this, right?

Let's get on then to the salutation.

The Salutation

Stifle the urge, no matter how well you know the person to whom your business letter is addressed, to refer to that person by any other name than is appropriate in business protocol. If the person's name is Cain (Exhibits 1 & 2), and you know him as your longtime friend – Candy — your salutation should still read, Dear Cain. There are even those that would maintain that the only salutation should properly be (from those same examples) Reverend Blackman.

Why is this?

Business letters are often read by others than those to whom the letter is addressed. In fact, it is common practice for business letters, particularly ones of importance, to be copied and distributed to other interested parties in the receiving organization. An inappropriate salutation could be construed as unwelcome or overt familiarity, lack of respect, a breach of business protocol, or...

Good advice: In business letters, play it straight, even if you are a born comedian.

There is one other salutation situation we should mention. That's the age-old question of what to do when you are writing a letter to more than one person in the same department or division. Granted, it doesn't happen very often, but it does happen, and when it does, people seldom know how to handle it. It gets sticky with the inside address and is just as sticky with the salutation.

When this situation arises on the inside address, we usually address the document first to the department head or the senior (in point of authority) individual in the situation. For example:

Mr. Harold D. Musgrave, Dir. of Purchasing
Mr. Lance Copeland, Senior Buyer
7K Cattle Feed Company Inc.
Broken Box, WY 88756

Sometimes, *Gentlemen* or *Dear Sirs* will work if you are 100 percent certain there are no women involved. But the term *Ladies* won't work in a similar situation for all women. If you are writing a letter to several women or both men and women, there is a way to handle it. You can avoid the salutation altogether.

How?

Simple. Start the letter without a salutation. We'll show you how that's done in a later section called *Letter Appearance and Forms.*

Let us say this about the salutation line in a business letter when there are several people and both sexes involved: There are no truly satisfactory guidelines. So whatever you do, you won't be wrong unless you use:

1.   "Ladies and Gentlemen," which sounds like the ring announcer at the Friday night fights.

2.   "Dear Sir or Madam," a salutation that sounds like you can't tell one sex from the other.

and

3.   "To whom it may concern," which sounds more like you're selling tickets to the Policeman's Ball or delivering handbills.

The Closing

When you are finally finished with this literary gem, you have to close it. This is called the complimentary closing.

It's been our experience that just about any closing — best regards, warmest regards, sincerely, cordially, respectfully — will do, if the closing is appropriate. If you are sending a letter to someone you barely know, *warmest regards* sounds a bit close to us.

Over the years, we have developed the habit of closing off with the words, "again, (person's name), thank you." It has been our experience that there are very few (if any) letters where this closing won't work in day-to-day business. However, we do recognize that there are professions where it would be entirely inappropriate.

Exhibit 3: Format And Features Of A Business Letter

Pin & Pen Press
6048 Orland Rd.
Angola, IN 46703

1 April 6, 1995

2

Mr. Dale Porter
678 Benton Road
Konger, MO 32323

Dear Mr. Porter: **3**

Thank you for your essay on senior writers. The distinctions you make between younger and older writers is fascinating.

4

We are just now completing our layout for the October issue. We are happy to inform you that both the theme and length of your essay lend themselves to the October issue.

A longer range view of our requirements for 1996 indicates a need for articles concerning management styles and practices in small to medium size companies. If you would be interested in these writing assignments, please let me know. I will be happy to give you more background information.

5   Again, Mr. Porter, thank you for your essay.

                              Best Wishes,

            6

                              Del Hammersmith

7   Enc. Check

Final Comments On The Business Letter Format

One last look at Exhibit 3 beginning on the previous page is enough to remind you of the seven key components of a good business letter:

1. Date.
2. Inside address.
3. Salutation.
4. Text.
5. Closing.
6. Signature block.
7. Enclosure(s).

Finally, Letter Appearance And Forms

According to the Administrative Management Society, there are a number of popular formats for business letters.

There is the *block* format where every line begins at the left margin. This is also the format you use when, for whatever reason, you decide to omit the salutation.

Another form is called the *semiblock* format in which the first sentence of each paragraph is indented. The *semiblock* generally is considered to be the most reader-friendly letter format.

Then there is what is called the *modified block*. The modified block is not widely used in business. What little appeal it does hold is primarily due to its rather liberal attitude toward punctuation. In this form, some paragraphs are blocked and italicized for emphasis.

The format you do use will in large measure determine how your letter looks. But other factors impact how a letter looks as well.

It should go without saying, that you always use high quality paper. Unless there is a good reason not to, use 20-pound, 8 1/2 x 11 white stationery. Remember, you not only want your readers to understand what you have written, you also want them to be able to read it with a minimum of hassle.

A 2-inch margin at the top is appropriate. A 1-inch margin at the sides and bottom is standard.

Edit, Edit, Edit, Edit, And, If Necessary, Revise

What do you do if you discover an error in a business letter you have written?

Exactly. You redo it. Nothing looks quite as bush league as a business letter with typographical errors or other minor problems.

Don't strike over, white out, or pencil in.

Don't do anything that will make you look less than professional.

Don't rely 100 percent on the systems built into your word processor. Even the grammar and thesaurus checks in your word processor will not necessarily spot missing punctuation, inappropriate word choice, improper tense, repetitious word usage, or awkward, muddy, and unclear sentences. In fact, there is only one way to double check the contents of your letter, and that is to proofread. Learn to proofread. Proofreading will improve your writing overnight.

Some Valid Generalizations About Business Letters

After more than 30 years of dealing with and thinking

about this subject of business letters, we've come to several conclusions that, no matter how harsh the glare or critical the examination, continue to hold up in the cold light of day.

The first conclusion is that business letters can be divided into two categories. First, there is the letter the business teachers like to call "the letter of enlightenment or understanding." These letters could just as easily be called letters of explanation or letters of *general interest*. Letters of explanation or general interest do just what the names imply: They explain things to the readers. More often than not, they explain, discuss, or detail neutral issues. In other words, these letters in general deal with issues, questions, matters, and circumstances which are of general interest and not likely to have either a significantly positive or negative impact on the reader.

The other type of letter comes under the heading of *specific interest*. These are letters that are designed to sell, persuade, or motivate. Consequently, it is more difficult to write a specific interest letter than a general one. After all, it is more difficult to persuade.

Think of it this way. Your general interest letter is a lot like the person who reads the news. Your specific interest letter is a lot like the person who interprets the news.

Now, having made that distinction, let's deal with a couple of other factors that directly impact how we write a business letter.

General interest business letters (to the public at large) are most effective when they are constructed for a reader with an average sixth grade level of reading comprehension. Sad, but true. On the other hand, if your general interest business letter is being sent out only to members of some specific professional group (e.g., engineers, doctors, lawyers), then aim your letter at the four-year college graduate level of comprehension (sixteen years of formal education).

If you were to apply this same thinking to the application and distribution of internal documents, you would be advised to design an internal document that is aimed at the twelfth grade level of comprehension. Communications experts have long held to the belief that if you are attempting to communicate with a healthy cross-section of the management side of corporate America, you should be drafting your document to a twelfth grade level of comprehension.

So, how do you do this?

If you are writing for a twelfth-grade level of reading comprehension, the average length of your sentences would be about 15 words and no more than 20 percent of the words you use would be longer than three syllables.

Writing for a sixth grade level? Temper the above. Make the sentences shorter and guard against sesquipedalianism.

Let us hasten to point out that what we've given you above is nothing more than a series of guidelines. If the above numbers intrigue you, you'll enjoy reading Robert Gunning's Techniques of Clear Writing.

Practical Practice #15

GENERAL BUSINESS LETTER EDITING. HOW MANY
WORDS CAN YOU TAKE OUT OF THIS EXAMPLE OF
AN EXTERNAL LETTER AND STILL ACCOMPLISH
YOUR OBJECTIVE?

Date   Your full name
                                       Your street address
                                       City, State Zip code

Recipient's full name
Institution or title
Institution (if title above)
Street address
City, State Zip code

Dear recipient's name:

The first paragraph should be brief. It should be straight to the
point. The recipient should be able to tell what the letter is
about after reading the first paragraph. A guideline to authoring
a tight, and effective first paragraph of a business letter is to
confine it to four sentences.

The second paragraph is broad in scope. Here is where you
define the totality of the situation. Mention relevant background
information. Explain or enlarge upon details that are important.
Detail qualifications, authority, scope of matter. Where
necessary, connect yourself to the matter being discussed. A

tightly written second paragraph of a general business letter can usually be accomplished in six sentences.

In the third paragraph you connect yourself and/or your interest, to the situation that is the focus of your letter. Focus is key to a well-written business letter. Don't stray from the main purpose of your letter. Straying from the central point of your letter may confuse the reader about your purpose for writing. If you want the reader to take some action, spell it out. Be certain you have avoided ambiguity. If any paragraph of your letter is going to be lengthy, the third paragraph is where you go into detail. Still, I would caution you to guard against being wordy or redundant.

The fourth paragraph (not always necessary) is brief. What do you expect? Is the course of action clear? Don't dawdle. Thank the recipient.

 closing
 SIGNATURE
 keyboarded name

enclosure (if necessary)

Effectiveness Of Your Letter

No matter the comprehension level of your reader or the purpose of your letter — to explain, sell, persuade, or motivate —the effectiveness is going to depend on the letter's:

1. Clarity.
2. Completeness.
3. Conciseness.
4. Correctness.
5. Credibility.

Let's deal with these elements one at a time.

LET'S START WITH CLARITY. If you can answer the following questions with an emphatic "yes," you have hurdled the clarity factor of a good business letter.

Is your letter easy to read? Does it flow? Are thoughts and ideas linked together? Is the focus maintained throughout the document? Have you avoided jargon, slang, vague business terms, and technical lingo? Is the reader familiar and comfortable with the language you're using? Have you given consideration to the layout of your letter: enough white space, avoidance of confusion, ease of understanding?

WHAT ABOUT COMPLETENESS? First of all, don't confuse brevity, conciseness, and completeness. You can achieve all three in the same document.

Let's start with these questions: Did you accomplish everything you intended when you sat down to author your document? Did you include everything that needed to be included? Do your readers have all the information they need for their actions? Have you anticipated and tried to answer your reader's more obvious questions? Hey, if being an effective business communicator were easy, you wouldn't have to wade through all of these considerations.

HOW ABOUT DOCUMENT CONCISENESS? One of the questions near and dear to our hearts because it is at the very core of the principle of *Write Tight and Right* is whether you expressed your thoughts in as few words as possible? Did you use the right words, the precise words? Did you write *oatmeal* instead of *breakfast*? Have you exaggerated or used superlatives when plain language, void of excessive adjectives, would be more effective? Have you purged your document of irrelevant material?

To achieve conciseness, you do all of the above and then you do one more thing: You do what you can to present your case without wasting the reader's time.

HOW ABOUT LETTER CORRECTNESS? How carefully have you edited your document? Are there any errors in grammar, punctuation, presentation, or spelling? How about the facts you have presented? Are they logically thought through? Finally — perhaps the most simple and important test of all — does the letter say what you want it to say? Or, now that you've re-read it, does it need further development to be completely accurate?

HAVE YOU MAINTAINED CREDIBILITY? Have you been fair? Have you represented your facts without slanting them? This is a key question and is at the heart of the issue of trust. That word *trust* has a lot to do with how your readers view your honesty and integrity and whether or not they will *buy* the case you have outlined. Will the data you have presented as being factual stand up under investigation and research? Have you said anything that could compromise either you or your company?

From Neutral Content To Matters Of 'Yes' And 'No'

Let's face it, it's easy to write a *yes* letter.

Any time you author a document that tells the reader exactly what the reader wants to hear, that letter is not going to be difficult to write. Why? Because when your readers open these letters, all their expectations are being met when they read what they want to see.

Do you recall the last time you received a check in the mail? Do you remember what happened?

Let us guess. You opened the letter, saw the check, read the amount of the check and, if it met your expectations, you perhaps read the letter later or maybe not at all. In some cases, the content of a *yes* letter, beyond the opening statement that your tax refund is enclosed, your invitation has been accepted, your promotion has been approved, or your mortgage application has been approved, is superfluous.

Yes letters start with the good news and then follow up with whatever needs to be said in order to conclude the matter. If any further explanation is needed, it should come after the favorable opening. The conclusion of the letter (like the salutation) employs standard business letter components.

The only problem with *yes* letters is that most of us don't get to author very many of them.

The 'No' Letter

The *no* letter is tougher to write. There just aren't very many palatable ways of saying *no*. It's one of those words no one wants to hear.

Unlike the *yes* letter where you blurt out the good news in the opening sentence of the opening paragraph, the most effective way of saying no and not rupturing your relationship with the individual, is to bury the *no* somewhere later in the letter.

The anatomy of a *no* letter is far more subtle than a *yes* letter. But, let's be honest, there is nothing you can do to hide the fact that it is a *no* letter. Generally the writer of such a letter starts by expressing concern or regret for the situation wherein the writer cannot give you a positive response. This is referred to as the *buffer*. It is intended to put the reader in as good a frame of mind as possible.

The second step in your *no* letter is usually an attempt to present the reader with the reasons why the answer can't be otherwise.

The third phase of the letter is the dreaded *no*.

The last phase of the *no* letter is usually an attempt by the author of the letter to get the reader's mind on something else. This effort means either an offer of something that will soften the blow of a negative response or a repeat of the logic leading to the *no*.

Exhibit #4: The 'No' Letter

Pin and Pen Press
6048 W. Orland Rd.
Angola, IN 46703

November 28, 1999

Mr. George Jacobs
121 West Main Street
Partridge, IL 67546

Dear Mr. Jacobs:

Your travel guide proposal for a feature article on the
100-year-old bed and breakfasts that dot the Michigan
coastline overlooking Lake Michigan has definite reader
appeal.

Unfortunately our travel editor has written a similar
article on the same subject that will appear in a pictorial
essay commemorating our 10th anniversary issue as
Michigan's most prestigious travel magazine. Because
of that, it would be inappropriate to run another article
on the same subject so soon after our anniversary issue.

Enclosed you will find a 32-page editorial guide which
pinpoints Pin and Pen Press' Travel Guide editorial
content for the next 18 issues. If you see a topic that

interests you, we invite contributions or inquiries.

Thank you for your continued interest in Pin and Pen Press.

Sincerely,

Matt Gaffer
Pin and Pen Press

The opening paragraph of the letter in Exhibit 4 attempts to prepare the recipient of this letter for the bad news that follows. The letter is saying that we like your idea but we've already done it. However, we like your style well enough to encourage you to try again.

EXHIBIT 5: THE 'YES' LETTER

Pin and Pen Press
6048 W. Orland Rd.
Angola, IN 46703

November 28, 1999

Mr. George Jacobs
121 W. Main St.
Partridge, IL 67546

Dear Mr. Jacobs:

Your travel guide proposal for a feature article on the 100-year-old bed and breakfast establishments that dot the Michigan coastline overlooking Lake Michigan is exciting. Our only question is when can you complete the article?

Our travel editor, Del Hammersmith, has requested that in addition to the article you also submit color pictorial layouts of the three or four inns you feel best lend themselves to this kind of presentation.

As indicated in our initial phone conversation, Pin and Pen Press pays $500 for a 2,000-word article and $50 for each photo used. Copy deadline for this article is

---

February 5, 2000.

If you have any questions, please contact me. Good luck on your assignment.

Sincerely,

Matt Gaffer
Pin and Pen Press

Despite the rather lengthy sentence structure, this letter works. The tone of this *yes* letter is as different as its structure. The good news is right up front. Then the writer fills in the relevant details.

The 'Specific' Interest Letter

Earlier in this section, we discussed the differences between a *general interest* and a *specific interest* letter. To that end, we have just devoted several minutes to the discussion of a letter whose primary purpose is to foster understanding or deliver straightforward, unbiased, or factual news. At the same time, we learned that the news contained in those letters can be good or bad, yes or no.

Now, however, we are entering a whole different realm: letters that attempt to sell, persuade, and motivate. This is

---

where that earlier distinction between someone who just reads the news and someone who interprets the news comes into play. In other words, our specific interest letter is somewhat more ambitious than its counterpart.

One question you may be asking yourself: Just exactly what is the difference between the two types of letters? Another question may well be how are they written differently?

To us, one of the most important distinctions between general and specific interest letters has always been the reader's attitude toward the letter. Most readers are open to reading general interest letters. Their attitude toward that letter may be casual ("I wonder what this is all about," "Gee, that's interesting," or "So what?"), or very focused ("I hope she says yes," or "If he says no, I'll be angry."). In either case, any attempt to manipulate the reader or the reader's views and attitudes is virtually nil.

Not so with the specific interest letter.

In the specific interest letter, the writer is charged with making the message interesting. This time around, it isn't enough just to get the reader to read the letter. No, you want your reader to do something as the result of reading your letter.

You want them to vote no on the new Sunday casino hours.

You want the reader to contribute to the library fund.

You want the reader to support you in the upcoming election.

Sometimes those *you wants* are hard to come by. In order to get them, you have to be clever, innovative, and — the hardest word of all to define — creative. So perhaps the best way to begin this rather challenging assignment is to focus on what you can do to make your letter interesting.

Interesting? To Do That, Start With Tone

The first element of a letter that makes it interesting to the reader is *tone*. Tone in letter writing is defined as the writer's attitude toward his reader. If the tone of the letter is natural, sincere, courteous, and helpful, the reader is going to be more receptive than the reader would be if the tone of the letter sounded contrived or if the reader felt that the writer had a haughty attitude. If your letter gives the reader the impression that you think you are in control, the reader will soon see that you won't be.

On this matter of tone, we believe that a letter that is more conversational and less formal tends to create more of a favorable acceptance than a formal letter approach. We also believe that one of the easiest ways to achieve the desired response from your reader is to present yourself in a fashion that will allow the reader to like you. People want to respond positively to people they like. But if your tone broadcasts the wrong signal, they will not respond, or at least not favorably.

Point number one then, in specific interest letters, is to project a courteous, helpful, and natural tone.

Sincerity Is Vital

A friend, who has demonstrated that he knows a great deal about writing, claims that character flaws like deceit, pretense, and hypocrisy are just as evident in a person's writing as they are in the person's behavior patterns. He then goes on to say that the traits of a person who is essentially honest, straightforward, and unaffected will likewise come through in their writing.

We tend to disagree.

From where we stand, the world is not that black and white.

You could be a straight-shooter of the first magnitude and still be a poor writer so that those admirable traits aren't projected through your writing. Those poor writing habits and what they imply could make you come across as something wholly undesirable.

If that is the case, **RULE #1** for projecting sincerity is to guard against the overuse of adjectives and superlatives. You've read letters written by people who are gushy or over enthusiastic. Ask yourself: Do you accept what those people say at face value? No one else does either.

RULE #2. Admit mistakes when you or your company have made them. If an apology is in order, make it. But make it brief. On the other hand, if you were right, don't gloat.

RULE #3. Always place the emphasis on constructive, forward looking, positive action.

The most sincere and, thus, effective writing is pleasant, direct, and straightforward without being the least bit contrived.

Be Conversational, Write Casually

The best advice we ever heard an old-timer give one of his young charges for constructing a no-nonsense business letter was this: "Write like you talk. Let your personality show through." The assumption here, of course, is that the writer doesn't have the personality of a wash cloth; there really is a personality to shine through.

Again, a caution. Have you heard the expression *stuffed shirt*? Of course, you have. Nowhere does the stuffed shirt element show through more than in a person's writing. Consider this:

> *Referring back to your letter of June 4, prior to the convention, we note that the estimated total expenditures for your party were well in excess of the actual $700 in expenses your group incurred during the duration of the three-day period.*

Instead, why not write:

> *Your total expenses were $700, considerably less than your estimate prior to the convention.*

Be natural, use your own words, talk with not at your reader, and be friendly.

Every Business Letter Should Try To Create Good Will

In addition to handling the situation that prompted the letter in the first place, your letter should:

1. Take the opportunity to make the recipient of the letter feel important.

2.　　　It should somehow encourage future business.

If your letter doesn't do these two things, then you haven't maximized the opportunity created by the situation.

Write Tight and Right Tip
THE NEXT TIME YOU WRITE A BUSINESS LETTER, STOP TO READ IT AFTER YOU HAVE DRAFTED THE OPENING SENTENCE. IF IT BEGINS WITH THE PRONOUN "I," STOP, TEAR UP WHAT YOU HAVE WRITTEN, AND START OVER. GETTING RID OF THE EGO "I" WILL GO A LONG WAY TOWARD MAKING THE RECIPIENT FEEL AS THOUGH YOU ARE TALKING "TO" HIM OR HER RATHER THAN "AT."

Exhibit 6:The 'Specific' Interest Letter:

Pin and Pen Press
6048 W. Orland Rd.
Angola, IN 46703

November 28, 1999

Mr. Harold Summers
Editor
Singer-Harris Publishing
2321 Tacoma
Anderson, NJ 10657

Dear Mr. Sommers:

<u>Deathscape</u> is a horror novel focusing on a large scale ecological disaster.

The story takes place in a coastal resort village and details the events leading up to a cataclysmic Labor Day disaster in which thousands perish.

An expanded synopsis of the manuscript of <u>Deathscape</u> is available upon request.

I look forward to your prompt expression of interest.

Sincerely,

Raymond T. Leffers

Enclosure

This is an excellent example of a tightly written business letter that addresses a specific interest. In this example, an author has addressed what is known as a query letter to the editor of a publishing company. He is attempting to interest the publisher in his recently completed novel.

The letter is brief, concise, and professional and contains everything that should be included in a letter of this nature.

1. The letter is directed to a specific individual. The spelling of the individual's name and the title have been checked.

2. The opening sentence is brief, to the point, and informative. The writer tells the recipient that his novel is horror fiction and it is based on a topical subject: ecology.

3. In an excellent sample of tight writing, the writer gives the editor abundant information: setting, timing, magnitude of the story — all things the editor will have to evaluate in order to determine whether or not his publishing company would be interested in working with this novel.

4. In the brief third paragraph, the writer sets the stage so that the editor can further develop the business relationship by informing him that the story is both available and for sale.

5. The letter closes with a gentle but professional prod that tells the editor, I'm a professional and you're professional. Let's handle this in a professional manner: promptly.

One last thing — and we shouldn't even mention this: You must make certain the letter is meticulously typed on letterhead stationery.

The package is professional.

The look is professional.

That's how you get a professional response.

And Finally

There is one facet of effective business communications, and particularly business writing, that cannot be condensed for the harried business person. Yet its mastery is an essential ingredient in the effective communications arsenal of anyone who hopes to be better than their run-of-the-mill counterpart. This magic ingredient is known as creativity.

Practical Practice #16

THROUGHOUT PART IV, WE HAVE TRIED TO SHOW YOU HOW DIFFERENT BUSINESS LETTERS WOULD LOOK IN A TIGHT AND RIGHT FORMAT. (SEE EXHIBITS #4, THE "NO" LETTER; #5, THE "YES" LETTER; AND #6, THE "SPECIFIC INTEREST" LETTER.) NOW, USING THE MODEL OF AN EFFECTIVE BUSINESS LETTER, WRITE A BUSINESS LETTER THAT REVOLVES AROUND THE FOLLOWING SITUATION:

1. You have decided to look for a new career opportunity and you have a specific company in mind.

2. You have learned that a friend is an employee of that company and she informs you that her employer is considering adding a new product manager in the company's marketing department.

3. You feel you are qualified for the position as she has described it.

4. You wish to demonstrate how prior work experience and your familiarity with similar types of products qualify you for such a position.

5. Be assertive. (Marketing is an assertive position.) Demonstrate a positive and confident attitude throughout the letter and close in a take-charge fashion.

"In the creative state, a man is taken out of himself. He lets down as it were a bucket into his subconscious, and draws up something which is normally beyond his reach. He mixes this thing with normal experiences and out of the mixture he makes a work of art."

— E. M. Forster

Another one of our mentors along the way made this distinction.

"There are two kinds of creativity: abstract and concrete. Abstract creativity is making something out of nothing. This is the stuff of art. Concrete creativity is making something that didn't exist out of something that already existed. This is the stuff of commerce."

— James K. Baker

It was Thomas Edison who said, "There's a better way to do it. Find it."

Can there be any doubt he was talking about creativity?

What we're talking about here is the one thing that cannot be taught. It can be encouraged, stimulated, and rewarded but it cannot be taught.

Creative application implies using ingenuity, cleverness, imagination, and sagacity to develop new solutions to often old, ordinary, and mundane problems.

Concrete creativity, readily recognized in research, problem solving, and decision-making is not always so evident in effective communication. It is likewise true that a clever way of expressing one's self is not always how concrete creativity most clearly manifests itself in writing. In fact, creativity is more likely to be found in business letters that focus on being interesting and informative to the reader. So how does a writer do this?

You start by making a commitment to learn the 3-I approach: the three things you must do when you sit down to write a business letter.

1. Identify with your reader.
2. Individuate your reader.
3. Inure your reader.

By simply mastering these three relatively simple steps, you can write letters that will make your readers view you as a person who is interested in not only their business but in them as individuals.

Identifying With Your Reader

When you identify with your readers, you are able to see things from their perspective. You may not share their point of view, but you can see how they came to their conclusions. You may not share their needs, but you recognize those needs in them as individuals. The same goes for desires and feelings.

In other words, you can imagine how they feel and anticipate how they will react.

When you are doing all of the above, you are identifying with your readers. In order to do this, you must master the delicate art of getting your own ego out of the way. You avoid using the pronoun *I*, and you learn to write your letters using the word *you*.

You (the reader) are my main concern.
You (the reader) are the focus of this letter.
My concern is what is good for you (the reader).
Your problem is what is important.

A caution.

Don't use the word you in every sentence, any more than you would the reader's name in every sentence. If you write:

How are you, Paul? I've been thinking of you, Paul.
Your problem, Paul, is the thing that concerns me most.
And, we'll find a way to solve it, Paul.

What happens?
It sounds phony, insincere, contrived, and corny.
It sounds just as phony if you substitute the pronoun *you* every time and every place we use the proper name, *Paul*. Once in those four sentences would be enough. Insert the *you* anywhere you think it will be most effective.
Bottom line: If you are genuinely concerned about an individual, it will show through in your writing. In this case, effective communication begins with cultivating a genuine concern for the people and the problems of the people.

Individuate Your Reader

By definition, when you individuate your reader, you separate that individual from all the others, no matter how similar he or she is to everyone else.

Again, how do you do that?

You personalize your letter whenever you have the opportunity. If the situation permits, try the "Dear Fred" approach as opposed to "Dear Mr. Johnson." This practice assumes, of course, that you would refer to the person by his first name in a telephone conversation or in person.

Another way is to use the person's name in the body of the letter; certainly no more than once. Even then, if it sounds contrived when you read it out loud, it probably is. Get rid of it.

One thing we've always done is to individually sign each letter, even if it is a mass mailing. It is a worthwhile personal touch, unless of course you are sending out 2,000 letters today.

When we know the person quite well (read that, done business with them in the past), we may go so far as to add a postscript of a personal nature. But, and this is the caution, never write a postscript related to the business described in the letter.

Why is individuating a letter important? Simple. It makes the recipient feel like the letter was written to him instead of the organization he or she represents.

There is one exception to all of this and that's the *bad news* letter. If you are drafting a letter to someone, and that letter is one you know the recipient does not want to receive, make that letter as impersonal as possible. This bad news comes from your organization to the recipient's organization. It is two entities, two *impersonal* things. Above all, it is not you, the individual, giving bad news to another individual.

Never is it more true that good news has many fathers, but bad news is an orphan.

Inure Your Reader

Desensitize what you have to say. Soften the blow. Make it easy as possible for the recipient of your document to accept the bad news: late delivery, credit problems, unsuccessful bid, whatever.

This is not easy to do. But it definitely is not as damaging as when you take a detached, *tough bananas* attitude toward the individual. A little compassion goes a long way.

Keep this in mind: Probably nowhere in the field of business writing does the art of writing a conversational-in-tone, friendly bad news letter come in more handy than when you separate the individual from the sins of the company. For example:

Bob, I know you probably weren't even aware of this, but your accounts payable people are more than 90 days behind. We haven't been paid for our May shipments. Now my people are telling me that if your firm doesn't get current, I'm going to have to sit on your September shipments.

Instead of calling Bob a deadbeat, you have exonerated him and separated him from the problem. Now he is likely to be your ally. He may even confide in you or become the conduit that gets your past due invoices paid.

The Last Word

Instant creativity is a virtual impossibility. The environment that nurtures creativity is different for each of us. Can you let yourself go? Will you allow yourself the mental latitude to dream? Are you willing to try something you never tried before?

The only thing that's holding you back is you.

Oh, yes, there is one more thing. As a final challenge, try rewriting the following:

Practical Practice #17

ABRAHAM LINCOLN DELIVERED THIS SPEECH, NOV. 19, 1863, AT THE SITE OF THE BATTLE OF GETTYSBURG IN PENNSYLVANIA. YES, WE KNOW IT; IT'S THE GETTYS-BURG ADDRESS. ELOQUENT AND BEAUTIFUL, IT STILL FALLS SOFTLY UPON THE EAR. BUT WHAT OF ITS MEAN-ING? CONSIDER THE FIRST-TIME LISTENER.

Original Version	Write Tight and Right Version
Four score and seven	_____
years ago our fathers brought forth	_____
on this continent, a new nation	_____
conceived in Liberty, and	_____
dedicated to the proposition	_____
that all men are created equal.	_____
Now we are engaged in a great	_____
civil war, testing whether that	_____
nation, or any nation so conceived	_____
and so dedicated, can long endure.	_____
We are met on a great battlefield	_____

of that war. We come to dedicate

a portion of that field as a final

resting place for those who gave

their lives that that nation might

live. It is altogether proper that

we should do this.

      But, in a larger sense, we

cannot dedicate —we cannot

consecrate — we cannot hallow —

this ground. The brave men, living

and dead, who struggled here have

consecrated it, far and above

our power to add or detract.

The world will little note, nor

long remember what we

say here, but it can never forget

what they did here. It is   _____

for us the living, rather, to   _____

be dedicated here to the   _____

unfinished work which they   _____

fought here have thus far so   _____

nobly advanced. It is rather   _____

for us to be here dedicated   _____

to the great task remaining   _____

before us that from these   _____

honored dead we take increased   _____

devotion to that cause for which   _____

they gave the last full measure   _____

of devotion that we here highly   _____

resolve that these dead shall not   _____

have died in vain — that this   _____

nation, under God, shall have   _____

a new birth of freedom — and   _____

that government of the people, by   _____

the people, for the people shall   _____

not perish from the earth.   _____

PART V

PRACTICE SOLUTIONS

Practical Practice #2 Solution

While every business situation may be different, here would be our expectations which would inform our planning:

1. We would develop two memos. One would go to all personnel. It would thank them for their understanding and cooperation at a difficult time. It would explain, in general, how the hours would be handled. All personnel would know their efforts were appreciated and how they would be paid. A second memo would go to all supervisors or others who would handle the paperwork and might receive additional questions. It would include a copy of the "Work Report and Absence Report" form. It would detail in 1-2-3 fashion the processing of both professional and union employee hours.

2. Certainly some form of communication is needed and should be sent as soon as possible upon the workers' return. Since confusion and rumor are possible, a written document is best. Personnel also need it for reference.

3. Personnel would be familiar with the distinction between professional personnel and union employees. The hours involved, known at the time, would need to be repeated. The form should be included in the memo to those processing it so no mistake can be made.

Practical Practice #3 Solution

1. Jimmy walked across the bridge, following the girl in the red dress. He stopped when she paused at the gate of the large house.

2. I explained to the girl the lesson was not as difficult as she thought. Her eyes filled with tears. Soon her body was racked with sobs.

3. Tom, Jim, Betty and Sally were going to the movie they thought began at 4:15 p.m. When they arrived at the theater, they found the earlier movie had started late. The new starting time for their movie was 5:15 p.m. instead.

4. The cousins took their sleds up the hill. Once there, they faced the sleds down the long slope and got on. Pushing off, they gathered speed as they passed the old oaken tree. They missed the long culvert and glided to a stop. That was just before the creek, swollen with water from the new, heavy snow.

5. He believed she should take the job if she really wanted. He was hesitant to say too much, however. She might think he was trying to unduly influence her decision. He didn't want to do that even though he had his own opinion.

Remember, these exercises could be changed in other ways. Yours may be better.

Practical Practice #4 Solution

The same memo written in an effective business style might read something like this.

Date:	9/09/99
To:	Jan Hawkins
From:	Carol Manning
Subject:	Cross Bow Investigation

We are four weeks behind schedule completing the initial phase of the investigation.

We are less than half finished with the Internal Audit, due the week of 9/13/99.
External Audit, due 9/20/99, is two weeks behind schedule.

Hennings is unable to give me a completion date.

Hanson has scheduled a meeting in her office at 2:00 on Friday, 9/13/99.

What was wrong with the first memo?

1.   It was one continuous paragraph. Hard for many people to read. We have corrected this by structuring the memo in four easy-to-read brief paragraphs focusing on the important information.

2.   Since this is an internal document, we have

Practical Practice #4 Solution (Cont.)

eliminated irrelevant information. For example: Since we have been assigned to this investigation, we know the timetable and (hopefully) we all know who the director is and where her office is located.

3. The coordinators of the project blamed their lack of progress on lack of available personnel. This makes them sound like they are offering excuses instead of reasons. It would be more appropriate to say, "unable to give you a completion date," and let it go at that. Their reasons for being late are best left to a discussion during the Friday meeting.

4. Meetings should be scheduled at a specific time, not left open to discussion. This is a time waster.

5. The text of the original memo contains 137 words. The revised memo contains 57. If time is money, then you have just saved more than half the cost of the original memo.

Practical Practice #5 Solution

1. Shivering, Kelly and I sat huddled. We knew we must protect ourselves from the cold of the coming arctic night.

2. My brother and I were born five minutes apart.

3. Scientists have searched nearly a century for a cure to the common cold.

4. When the alien space ship landed at midnight in our backyard, no one in the family knew what to do. However, my younger sister Mary was the only one to be hysterical.

5. To demonstrate agility, the contestant had to put one block on another, ride a tricycle, pull a string through a hole, and walk on a straight line.

6. The speed of the Indianapolis Memorial Day 500-mile race is reduced because of an average of six caution flags, three wrecks, and one spectator injury. *These obstacles test the drivers' skills and the cars' endurance.* (Understood?)

Practical Practice #6 Solution

Beautiful	lovely, comely, good-looking, stunning, ravishing, gorgeous
Careless	nonchalant, unconcerned, casual, offhand, negligent, thoughtless
Decent	credible, decorous, pure, acceptable, reasonable, tolerable
Emotion	sentiment, passion, sensibility, sensation, feeling, affection
Fantasize	dream, muse, imagine, envision, visualize, fancy
Gloomy	sad, melancholy, pessimistic, cheerless, dejected, doleful
Hard	firm, rigid, strong, callous, impermeable, severe
Ignorant	inexperienced, unaware, blind, incomprehensible, superficial, bewildered
Joy	happiness, delight, gaiety, mirth, pleasure, cheerfulness
Kiss	smooch, peck, smack, caress, graze, brush
Liberty	freedom, emancipation, privilege, license, independence, permission
Mad	crazy, insane, rabid, frantic, turbulent, enrage
Necessary	obligation, requirement, need, demand, essential, indispensable
Opinion	idea, thought, belief, conviction, theory, tenet

Practical Practice #6 Solution (Cont.)

Partial	incomplete, fractional, unfinished, biased, partisan, prejudiced
Question	problem, query, interrogation, doubt, dispute, challenge
Refuse	nonacceptance, deny, decline, reject, repudiate, exclude
Sad	sorrowful, downcast, dejected, unhappy, woeful, depressed
Tarnish	taint, dishonor, stain, sully, besmirch, defame
Unfair	unjust, unreasonable, unequal, inequitable, unsporting, discriminatory
Walk	ramble, stroll, promenade, saunter, march, tramp
Yield	crop, harvest, product, surrender, cede, acquiesce
Zero	nothing, naught, none, blank, nobody, nonentity

Practical Practice #7 Solution

Cold sweat	nervous
Cool as a cucumber	calmly
Cradle of the deep	asleep
Crow to pick	problem
Daily repast	meal
Dead as a doornail	dead
Dead giveaway	obvious
Depths of despair	discouraged
Die is cast	decision
Dog days	sweltering
Doomed to disappointment	certain failure
Down my alley	my style
Draw the line	stop
Drown one's sorrows	drinking
Fish out of water	awkward
Each and every	all
Ear to ground	listen
Exception proves the rule	rarely happens
Eyes of the world	everyone
Face the music	take responsibility
Fast and loose	oblivious
Feather in her cap	honor
Fill the bill	precisely
Filthy lucre	money
Flash in the pan	promising but disappointing

Practical Practice #7 Solution (Cont.)

Fly off the handle	angry
Fools rush in	reckless
First and foremost	first
Get the upper hand	control
Clear as mud	confusing
Get what I mean?	understand?
Gild the lily	unnecessary
Grain of salt	skeptical

Practical Practice #8 Solution

1. Early on, we had an uneasy feeling when we stumbled upon an abandoned campsite.

2. My report covers my life's most traumatic event, one which I hope you never experience.

3. When I asked who had called, I was told it was my father.

4. With our out-of-control car heading directly at a tree, the three of us yelled and prayed.

5. Neither I nor the other driver was injured seriously although our cars were totally wrecked.

Remember, these exercises could be changed in other ways. Yours may be better.

Practical Practice #9 Solution

1.   The 10 a.m. launch, delayed a day by NASA (National Aeronautics and Space Administration), now had only a 50-minute weather window.

2.   Without falling, Bob regained his balance and said, "There's nothing to it."

3.   Out of the corner of his eye, Tom saw her walk up the lane. He knew the felled tree was his coup de maitre. It could also be coup be maitre.

4.   I asked him if he knew the solution.

5.   Bob asked, "Do you know who said 'A penny saved is a penny earned'?"

6.   If I had earned my master of business administration as our vice president did, I would not have been in this for 12 years.

7.   The Johnson's house was for sale.

8.   I am sure you know John Tyler, our director of off-shore properties.

9.   We had three chances: (1) sell, (2) wait, or (3) buy more.

Practical Practice #9 Solution (Cont.)

10.   Can this self-tightening locknut be ordered?

11.   It was the easier course.

12.   He asked if I could get tickets for the highly acclaimed show, <u>Phantom of the Opera</u>. (Or it could be *Phantom of the Opera*.)

13.   A.G. Smith, my cousin, asked two questions.

14.   You know our plan: keep talking.

15.   "'If once you fail, try, try again' is a good quote for our use," I said to the superintendent.

Practical Practice #10 Solution

The second paragraph should begin with the sentence, "The officers have decided on the following draft plan" on the fourth line. Reason: It introduces a shift in emphasis from the time involved to how the plan will be prepared.

The third paragraph should begin with the sentence in the 7th line, "San Francisco Vice President John Haller will be in charge of the draft team." Reason: This paragraph and the two that follow it could be part of the second paragraph which introduces the proposal draft plan. It follows logically to do so, since these sentences amplify the plan. However, it would make a lengthy paragraph.

The fourth paragraph would begin with the sentence in the 11th line, "The revision team will be led by New York City Vice President Sandra Lolich." Reason: We now have shifted from the San Francisco draft team to the New York City revision team.

The fifth paragraph would begin with the sentence in the 13th line, "When the revision team has completed its work, the final evaluation team will be composed of Haller, Lolich, and President Tim Merritt." Reason: We now have shifted to the work of the evaluation team. As we indicated earlier, an argument could be made for keeping paragraphs three, four, and five as part of paragraph two. We have two reasons not to do so. It would make a long paragraph and we like shorter paragraphs!

Practical Practice #10 Solution (Cont.)

The sixth paragraph would begin with the sentence in the 16th line, "In the meantime, the cooperation of all personnel in completing this project is appreciated." Reason: Obviously, the emphasis has shifted, suggested by the transitional phrase "In the meantime."

We would make "Your hard work is necessary and valued!" the last and separate paragraph to emphasize it (note the !). It also could be argued that it goes with the preceding paragraph because of its content.

So, you see in some cases it is quite clear where paragraph breaks come. In some others, it depends a bit on what you are trying to emphasize.

Practical Practice #11 Solution

Please do not hesitate to call	call
Pursuant to our agreement	according to
Reached the conclusion	concluded
Seldom if any	rarely
Please sign on the designated line	sign here
This is to inform you	note
Until such time as	when
We ask your kind permission	request
We wish to acknowledge	confirm
We would like to ask	ask
Will be kind enough	please
Despite the fact that	despite
Due to the fact that	because
In this day and age	today
Kindly be advised	note
In the near future	soon
A large number of	many
It is circular in shape	round
At the present time	now
At a later date	later
Are of the opinion that	believe
At all times	always
Attached please find	attached
Made the announcement that	told

Practical Practice #12 Solution

1. Times, page numbers, money, measures, percentages.
2. False. It usually is, not always.
3. Yes. 75,000,000 or 75 million.
4. 2,000,000,000,000. 2,000,000,000,000,000.
   2,000,000,000,000,000,000.
5. Numerals. 0.45 or 0.6.
6. A.
7. Write it out.
8. A.
9. Spell it out.
10. Time.
11. False. There are two.
12. False. Write it out.
13. True.

Practical Practice #13 Solution

As with all our examples, there is more than one way to author these solution documents. However, this example does demonstrate the principle of tight writing in an internal document.

This document presents the author with a somewhat different problem. The author is communicating with several different levels of employee, not just his immediate staff, which already understand the situation. In other words, the policy has to be drafted in such a fashion that all levels of employment understand. Here, the author makes no assumptions about prior knowledge. The statement must be straightforward.

SEXUAL HARASSMENT POLICY

Sexual harassment will not be tolerated.

Sexual harassment is defined as any verbal or physical act which causes an employee to feel uncomfortable in any company/business related activity.

If an employee feels that he/she is being sexually harassed, the incident should be reported to the Human Resources Manager immediately.

In a broadly stated policy such as a sexual harassment policy, there is wisdom in not offering examples. Examples in such matters can be restrictive. In other words, if it's not on the list, it isn't sexual harassment. That is clearly a situation you want to avoid. Let time and reported incidents sort out the direction.

Practical Practice #14 Solution

CONFIDENTIAL

Date: 04/06/99

To: P. George Miller
            William Phillips
            Gordon Roberts
            Gerald Timmons

From: M.M. Durning

Subject: Proposed Correction Plan

You are all aware that our company has experienced a significant decline in sales over the last two quarters. At the same time, scrap rates are up, absenteeism has increased, quality has dipped, and daily as well as weekly production rates have dropped.

To compound matters, Fedrayco, our largest customer, is now projecting significantly reduced fourth-quarter product requirements. This cutback, Fedrayco informs us, is the result of three straight months of shipments exceeding the .02% AQL tolerance standard called for in the purchase agreement. It should be pointed out that Fedrayco production continues at an all-time high.

In light of the above and following my discussions with each of you, I will be instituting a series of changes. These changes are

Practical Practice #14 Solution (Cont.)

designed to rectify our current operational problems as well as tighten procedures.

Effective 04/15/96, etc. ... (At this point the author of the document may choose two approaches.)

    1. List the corrective actions, the changes in policy, and the proposed timing for the changes in the original document.

    2. List them in a separate document to be issued at a later (but soon after) date.

Let's look a little closer at our example.

1.   First of all, the nature of this report is confidential because it deals with matters you do not want discussed outside of the management level of the company.

2.   Once again, the author of this document leans on the principle of reinforcement.
        I'm going to tell you what I'm going to tell you.
        Then ... I'm going to tell you.
        Then ... I'm going to tell you what I told you.

The author at this point is in the "I'm going to tell you" phase of communication. She has held a round of discussions with each of her department heads (first phase) and now she is informing them (by means of this document) that something is going to happen. The third phase, of course, would be the corrective actions document, which spells out the actions the president wants taken.

Practical Practice #14 Solution (Cont.)

3.   This is an internal document. It uses a memo format, and it can be constructed in a number of different ways. One way, of course, is to begin with a kind of explanatory/summary text similar to that presented in the example. This is a more subtle approach. This document could then continue with a list of corrective actions and a timetable for implementation — all in one document. The disadvantages to this approach is that some of the more subtle changes may be overlooked.

Another approach would be to inform your staff that changes are forthcoming, introducing those reforms in separate documents at programmed intervals. The primary disadvantage to this approach is that employees may embrace the old "waiting for the other shoe to drop" attitude. Plus, with this letter approach, it takes longer to get necessary changes implemented.

The last phase (Then I'm going to tell you what I told you) section of whichever approach you decide must be the most effective in communicating with your managers because it contains the fully detailed plan for action. It will be complete with trigger dates and the corrections you have agreed to implement. Plus, it will provide the documentation each department head needs to spell out action plans for that staff and subordinates.

Practical Practice #15 Solution

Date

Your full name
Your street address
City, State Zip code

Recipient's full name
Institution or title
Institution (if title above)
Street address
City, State Zip code

Dear recipient's name:

The first paragraph should be brief. ~~It should be straight~~ and to the
point. The recipient should ~~be able to tell~~ know what the letter is

about after ~~reading~~ the first paragraph. A guideline to

~~authoring~~ a tight, and effective first paragraph ~~of a business~~

~~letter~~ is to confine it to four sentences.

The second paragraph is broad. ~~in scope.~~ Here is where you

define ~~the totality of~~ the situation. Mention relevant

background information. Explain or enlarge upon important

Practical Practice #15 Solution (Cont.)

details. ~~such as that are important~~. Detail qualifications, authority, scope of matter. Where necessary, connect yourself. ~~to the matter being discussed~~. A tightly written second paragraph ~~of a general business letter~~ usually can be accomplished in six sentences.

In the third paragraph you connect yourself ~~and/or your interest~~, to the situation. ~~that is the focus of your letter.~~ ~~Focus is key to a well-written business letter~~. Don't stray from the main purpose of your letter. ~~Straying from the central point of your letter may confuse the reader about your purpose for writing~~. If you want ~~the reader to take~~ some action, spell it out. ~~Be certain you have~~ Avoid ambiguity. If any paragraph ~~of your letter~~ is going to be lengthy, it's the third. ~~paragraph is where you go into detail. Still, I would caution you to guard against~~

Practical Practice #15 Solution (Cont.)

~~being wordy or redundant~~.

The fourth paragraph (not always necessary) is brief. What do you expect? Is the course of action clear? ~~Don't dawdle~~.

Thank the recipient.

closing
SIGNATURE
keyboarded name

enclosure (if necessary)

Practical Practice #16 Solution

May 7, 1999

George R. Miller
3127 Randalia St.
Milbourne, IA 61285
421-795-6432

Andrew Stern
Director of Human Resources
Morrison Steel Fabricating, Inc.
42 Commerce Way
Tantaty, OK 76764

Dear Mr. Stern:

Recently I spoke with Linda Rogers of your Quality Assurance Department. She informed me that you are considering adding a marketing manager for CRCQ automotive stampings in your fabricated metals division. As a marketing manager with extensive experience in the field of metal stampings, I am well qualified for such a position.

For the past ten years, my responsibility has been the introduction and launching of new product lines. These introductions have ranged from pre-fab architectural stampings to high volume automotive parts. During this period, I managed a field sales force of forty-five manufacturer's representatives and an internal staff of fifteen. This experience, coupled with a strong academic background — BS in Mechanical Engineering and an MBA from Tufston — enabled me to launch each product line on time and under budget.

Practical Practice #16 Solution (Cont.)

My greatest successes, however, have come in the arena of automotive parts. Of four automotive products launched during the last ten years, three are currently running ahead of profit projections, and the fourth, still in its first year, will be profitable in its second year on the market. I am confident I can deliver the same kind of strong product performance profile for Morrison Steel Fabricating. I will be happy to discuss my marketing methodology with you at a suitable time and location.

I have enclosed my resume for your further consideration. I will call you within the next two weeks to see if we can arrange a mutually convenient time for an interview. If you wish to contact me before that time, I can be reached at _____ after 7:00 p.m.

Thank you,
SIGNATURE
keyboarded name

enclosure

Practical Practice #16 Solution (Cont.)

As with all of our applied examples, the previous letter serves only as a model.

1. The first paragraph is brief, introduces the applicant, and states the purpose of the letter. It accomplishes all of these purposes in three sentences.

2. The second paragraph is broad in scope, covering the letter writer's experience in both sales and marketing as well as related management experience. Note that it also covers the applicant's education and how it relates to his qualifications.

3. The third paragraph shows how that prior experience qualifies the writer for the new position.

4. Finally, the fourth paragraph informs the recipient that more action (request for an interview) can be expected.

5. Note that the closing is a simple "thank you."

How does your letter compare?

AFTERWORD

It's obvious we haven't covered everything you need to know about effective business writing. You can take some solace in realizing the authors continue to learn, just as you are learning, and we've been at the task for decades. The truth is that no one ever knows everything needed in a field that — like all of life today — changes from day to day.

But keep in mind the one central point we've tried to make: The key is to make your writing tight and right. No better way exists to make it tight than to write short sentences. No better way exists to make it right than to keep working at it. If you take most - not all, but most - of your long sentences and make two and if you commit yourself to improvement, you're probably doing what you need.

One other positive about continuing to work at your writing improvement. Recent research confirms that a critical part in slowing the aging process is to stay mentally active. So if you always are at work thinking about your writing, thinking about communicating more effectively, thinking about ways to write tight and right, you're more likely to stay as young as we are!

NOTES

9 780964 560635